BAKE & SPRINKLE

CHAHRAZAD AL HAJJAR

FRONT TABLE BOOKS
AN IMPRINT OF CEDAR FORT, INC.
SPRINGVILLE, UTAH

To Adam and Lana, I hope this book
inspires you to always follow your dreams.

To Sami, for believing in me.

ISBN 13: 978-1-4621-4279-8

Published by Front Table Books, an imprint of Cedar Fort, Inc.
2373 W. 700 S., Springville, UT 84663
Distributed by Cedar Fort, Inc., www.cedarfort.com

Library of Congress Control Number: 2022938813

Edited by Celia Gallup
Cover design and interior layout and design by Shawnda T. Craig
Cover design © 2022 Cedar Fort, Inc.

Printed in the United States of America

10 9 8 7 6 5 4 3 2 1

Printed on acid-free paper

CONTENTS

MY STORY

Welcome to my first baking cookbook!

I love baking, especially when my cakes taste as good as they look! My biggest joy is when I see people's reactions when they taste my desserts. In this book, I am sharing all of my tried and tested recipes with you so you can create beautiful memories in your kitchen.

With all the lifestyle changes we have witnessed over the past two years, baking has become a regular activity in so many people's lives. Families have been spending more time together than ever before and, as a result, more time in the kitchen creating and enjoying meals together.

First, let me tell you more about my baking journey. I have been baking for over nine years and sharing my creations with an audience from all over the world through my social media page "@chahrazadscuisine" on Instagram and more recently on TikTok and Youtube. I started my page "Chahrazad's Cuisine" in 2013. I was a new, full-time working mom . At the beginning, I shared the recipes I was making for my family on a daily basis. Then, I began to bake simple desserts, such as cookies for a bake sale at work or a two-layered chocolate cake for a barbecue night with friends. Later, I took a basic cake decorating class which taught me the basics of making American buttercream and piping. The real learning, though, happened in my small apartment kitchen in Dubai every single night after work and after my son went to sleep. There, I would bake, experiment, and, at many times, get frustrated. I learned everything through trial and error and with the support of many taste testers around me, including my husband, brothers, colleagues, and friends.

Throughout my baking journey, I have had several appearances and continue to regularly appear on local and regional food channels where I share delicious recipes and teach others how to enjoy their time in the kitchen. In 2020, I launched my own Sprinkles line, Pinkles. That same year, I also started giving online baking classes for the first time. I taught hundreds of baking enthusiasts from all over the world how to bake different desserts.

When I started my baking journey nine years ago, I never found a central source of information that provided all the recipcs and basic skills required for a new baker. That is what encouraged me to write a book and share my knowledge so that bidding bakers can find a single source of all the information they need for baking success. Every single recipe in this book has been carefully crafted and includes clear measurements and detailed step-by-step instructions to make your baking journey as smooth and fun as possible.

Whether you want to just bake your husband's or child's next birthday cake, prepare a stunning dessert for your next family dinner party, or have foolproof recipes for your baking business, there are so many recipes for you in this book. I want you to succeed in your baking journey, to bake and impress, and, most importantly, to enjoy the whole process.

I hope you enjoy trying out these recipes as much as I enjoy baking them in my kitchen every day.

Happy baking!

—Chahrazad

BAKING ESSENTIALS

Baking and Cake Decorating Tools

Here are the tools you should invest in if you are planning on baking:

- MIXER: You can use either an electric mixer with a hand beater or a stand mixer. If you can invest in a stand mixer, it will make things much easier for you.

- KITCHEN SCALE: This tool is essential for successful baking and getting consistent results. I highly recommend investing in one. This book provides both metric and cup measurements. If you do have a kitchen scale, I suggest you follow the metric measurements provided in each recipe.

- ROUND CAKE PANS: Most of the cake recipes in this book can be made in any cake pan size. However, I would recommend following the cake pan size indicated in each recipe for best results. A good quality metal cake pan will contribute toward a great cake texture.

- MEASURING SPOONS: These are essential for measuring ingredients such as vanilla extract, salt, baking powder, and baking soda.

- MIXING BOWLS: In addition to the bowl of the stand mixer, you need at least one additional mixing bowl for measuring dry/wet ingredients separately.

- FINE SIEVE: This is essential for sifting your dry ingredients in several of these recipes.

- rubber spatula: This is used for scraping down the sides of the mixer bowl. It is useful when making macarons or buttercream.

- SMALL SAUCEPAN: This is required when making swiss meringue buttercream, caramel, or homemade custard.

- PARCHMENT PAPER/ROUNDS: Parchment paper should be used when baking cookies. For cakes, I usually use pre-cut parchment rounds.

- COOKIE SHEETS: Non-stick cookie sheets are usually a certain thickness that helps cookies maintain shape and not burn during baking.

- ICE CREAM SCOOP: This will be used to achieve a consistent shape and size when you are baking cookies.

- ROLLING PIN: This is required for rolling cookie or tart dough.

- COOKIE CUTTERS: These are useful when making cookie shapes for desserts like sugar cookies.

- DIGITAL THERMOMETER: To ensure food safety, this is required when making a meringue-based buttercream.

- COOLING RACK: This is important for cooling cake layers and cookies.

For decorating layered cakes, the following tools are essential:

- Bread Knife (for trimming cake tops)
- Cake Turntable
- Non-Slip Mat
- Cake Scraper/Smoother
- Offset Spatula (small or large depending on preference)
- Piping Bags
- Piping Tips
- Acrylic Disc
- Tall Cake Scraper/Smoother (I prefer using the metal ones)

CORE INGREDIENTS

Do you ever come home craving some cookies for yourself or your kids and then get frustrated that you do not have all the required ingredients? I always make sure to have the following ingredients in my pantry and fridge so that I can bake almost anything that comes to mind when a craving hits.

- All-Purpose Flour
- Self-Rising Flour
- Cake Flour
- Baking Soda
- Baking Powder
- Unsweetened Cocoa Powder
- Salt
- Unsalted Butter
- Neutral Oil (I use Canola Oil)
- Vanilla Extract
- Eggs

- Whole Milk
- Whipping Cream
- Coffee
- Chocolate Chips
- Fine Sugar
- Powdered Sugar
- Almond Flour (for making macarons)
- White Vinegar (for wiping bowls in some recipes)
- Baking Spray
- Corn Syrup

OTHER INGREDIENTS

These ingredients are nice to have if you want to play around with flavors and for decorating desserts:

- Lemon Extract
- Almond Extract
- Cinnamon
- Sprinkles

- Gel Food Coloring
- Oil Based Coloring (for coloring chocolate)
- Edible Gold Luster Dust
- Gold Leaf

BAKING TIPS

Here are my top 10 tips for baking delicious and beautiful cake layers:

- Use room temperature ingredients: Milk, butter, and eggs should always be at room temperature when baking a cake. Unless specified otherwise in any of the recipes, always take them out of the fridge at least 1 hour before you want to start baking. However, when baking cookies, it is best to use cold eggs.

- Grease your cake pans with baking spray, and line them with parchment rounds: This will ensure the cakes come out easily when cooled, especially very moist cakes that tend to stick (such as the vanilla cake in this book).

- Preheat the oven 30 minutes before preparing the cake batter: Cake batter needs a hot oven in order to rise nicely.

- Place the cake pans in the center of the oven: If your oven is small, bake only two cake pans at a time.

- Use a kitchen scale to split the cake batter evenly among the cake pans being used.

- Never open the oven in the first 20 minutes of baking.

- Always set a timer to the time called for in the recipe: This will ensure you do not forget the cake you worked hard on preparing.

- Let the cakes cool in the pans before inverting them onto a wire rack: Resist the urge to remove the cakes while they are still hot.

- Do not overmix the cake batter and do not overbake the cake: Following these two tips will help you achieve fluffy and soft cake layers.

- The cake is ready when a toothpick inserted in the center comes out clean or the cake starts to shrink around the edges of the pan.

CONVERSION CHART

Volume		Weight		Temperature	
U.S.	Metric	U.S.	Metric	°F	°C
1 tsp.	5 mL	½ oz.	15 g	250	120
1 Tbsp.	15 mL	1 oz.	30 g	300	150
¼ cup	60 mL	3 oz.	90 g	325	160
⅓ cup	80 mL	4 oz.	115 g	350	180
½ cup	125 mL	8 oz.	225 g	375	190
⅔ cup	160 mL	12 oz.	350 g	400	200
¾ cup	180 mL	1 lb.	450 g	425	220
1 cup	250 mL	2¼ lb.	1 kg	450	230

LAYER CAKES

Every cake has a story to tell!

CHOCOLATE CAKE 9 • VANILLA CAKE 12

CARAMEL CAKE 14 • FRUITY PEBBLES CAKE 17

LEMON CAKE 20 • NEAPOLITAN CAKE 22

RED VELVET CONFETTI CAKE 25 • COOKIES & CREAM CAKE 28

ALMOND CAKE 30 • CHOCOLATE YELLOW CAKE 32

BLACK FOREST CAKE 34 • PEANUT BUTTER & CHOCOLATE CAKE 36

CHOCOLATE ORANGE CAKE 39 • PUMPKIN SPICE CAKE 42

TRIPLE CHOCOLATE CAKE 45 • VICTORIA SPONGE CAKE 48

COCONUT CUSTARD CAKE 50 • VANILLA & BLACKBERRY COMPOTE CAKE 52

STRAWBERRY SHORTCAKE 54 • BOSTON CREAM PIE CAKE 56

CARROT CAKE 58 • ICE CREAM BIRTHDAY CAKE 60

CHOCOLATE CAKE

Makes one two-layer 8-inch cake

Who doesn't love a decadent and moist chocolate cake? This recipe results in a delicious homemade chocolate cake that everyone will love. Nothing beats a classic Chocolate Cake with a delicious Chocolate Frosting.

CHOCOLATE CAKE

2 cups (250g) all-purpose flour

2 cups (400g) sugar

¾ cup (75g) cocoa powder

2 teaspoons baking powder

1½ teaspoons baking soda

1 teaspoon salt

1 cup (240ml) full fat milk

½ cup (125ml) vegetable oil

1 cup (240ml) hot water (or coffee)

2 eggs

2 teaspoons vanilla extract

Chocolate Sprinkles (for decoration)

CHOCOLATE FROSTING

1½ cups (339g) unsalted butter, softened

2 tablespoons full fat milk

1 teaspoon vanilla extract

2¼ cups (281g) icing sugar

255g semi-sweet chocolate chips

CHOCOLATE CAKE

1. Preheat the oven to 180°C (350°F). Spray 2 8-inch round cake pans with baking spray and line the bottom with parchment rounds.

2. Measure the flour, sugar, cocoa powder, baking powder, baking soda and salt. Sift using a fine sieve into the bowl of a stand mixer.

3. In a separate bowl, measure the milk, oil, and hot water. Add in the eggs one at a time mixing well after each addition. Add the vanilla extract and mix.

4. Add the wet ingredients mixture to the dry ingredients. Then, using the paddle attachment, mix them just until combined.

5. Stop the mixer. Scrape down the sides and the bottom of the mixer bowl and mix again for a few seconds just until combined. Divide the batter evenly among the cake pans using a kitchen scale.

6. Bake 20-25 minutes or until a toothpick inserted in the center of the cake comes out clean.

7. Let the cakes cool for 20 minutes in the pans before inverting onto a wire rack to cool completely.

8. Wrap the cake layers individually in plastic wrap and chill in the fridge overnight before decorating.

CHOCOLATE FROSTING

1. Melt the chocolate chips in a heat proof bowl in the microwave for 30 second intervals (Start with 30 seconds, stir the chocolate and then heat for another 30 seconds and so on until the chocolate has almost fully melted). Stir to melt completely. Set aside to cool.

2. In the bowl of a stand mixer fitted with the paddle attachment, cream the butter until pale and fluffy for about 3-4 minutes.

3. Add the milk and mix. Add the melted chocolate and mix until well combined. Add the vanilla extract and mix.

4. Add the icing sugar all at once beating on low speed at first until they are combined. Then, beat on high speed for 4-5 minutes before reducing the speed to the lowest setting and letting it mix for 5 minutes. This will help remove most of the air bubbles.

ASSEMBLY

1. Fill a large piping bag with the Chocolate Frosting (no piping tip needed). Trim the tops of the cake layers using a serrated (bread) knife. Place a nonslip mat on a cake turntable. Top with a large cake board (to help lift the cake easily). Add a small amount of buttercream and then place a cake board the same size of the cake.

2. Start filling and layering the cake. Once done, frost the top and sides of the cake with the first layer (crumb coat) of frosting and chill for at least 30 minutes. Once chilled, frost the top and sides of the cake with another generous layer of the frosting and smooth using a tall cake scraper. You can cover the cake top with chocolate sprinkles.

3. Chill until ready to serve.

VANILLA CAKE

Makes one three-layer 6-inch cake

Having a go-to vanilla cake recipe is a must for anyone interested in baking regularly. However, it is not easy to find a delicious and fluffy vanilla cake recipe. This recipe results in tasty vanilla cake layers that are moist, yet firm enough for decoration. It can be paired with literally any frosting flavor that comes to your mind. I usually pair it with my vanilla Swiss meringue buttercream, and it always impresses even the pickiest eater.

VANILLA CAKE

1½ cups (170g) self-rising flour

1¼ cups(150g) all-purpose flour

1 cup full fat milk

1 tsp. vanilla extract

1 cup (226g) unsalted butter, softened

2 cups (400g) sugar

4 eggs

VANILLA SWISS MERINGUE BUTTERCREAM

200g egg whites (from 6 large eggs)

1½ cups (300g) sugar

1¾ cups (400g) unsalted butter,
    softened

½ tsp. vanilla extract

VANILLA CAKE

1. Preheat the oven to 350°F (180°C). Spray three 6-inch pans round pans with baking spray and line the bottom with parchment rounds.

2. Combine both flours and set aside. Mix the milk and vanilla and set aside.

3. In the bowl of a stand mixer fitted with the paddle attachment (or using an electric mixer), cream the butter for 3 minutes until smooth and fluffy.

4. Scrape down the sides, add the sugar, and beat for another 2-4 minutes. Add the eggs one at a time, mixing well after each addition.

5. Add the flour mixture gradually in three parts, alternating with the milk and vanilla and mixing well after each addition.

6. Scrape down the sides and the bottom of the mixer bowl and mix again for a few seconds just until combined. Divide the cake batter evenly among the 3 pans using a kitchen scale.

7. Bake for 25-30 minutes or until a toothpick inserted in the center of the cake comes out clean.

8. Let the cakes cool completely in the pans before moving onto a wire rack. Wrap the cake layers in plastic wrap and chill in the fridge overnight before frosting and decorating.

VANILLA SWISS MERINGUE BUTTERCREAM

1. Wipe all the tools you will be using with white vinegar.

2. Using a kitchen scale, measure the egg whites before transferring them to a saucepan.

3. Add the sugar to the egg whites. Place the saucepan over medium heat and stir. Do not leave the pan while stirring. Use a candy thermometer to measure the mixture's temperature. Once it reaches 150°F, take the saucepan off the heat immediately.

4. Transfer the mixture to a mixer bowl fitted with the whisk attachment and whisk it on medium/high speed until the mixture turns white and glossy and forms stiff peaks. This is the meringue stage (when you lift the whisk up, the mixture does not fall off and has a pointy peak).

5. Slowly start adding the butter, one cube at a time until it has all been added in. Keep mixing. At this point, you can switch to the paddle attachment.

6. The mixture may turn crumbly. Keep mixing, and it will eventually turn into a silky-smooth buttercream.

7. Add the vanilla extract and mix to combine. Reduce the mixer speed to the lowest speed and let the buttercream mix for about 5 minutes. This will reduce most of the air bubbles.

ASSEMBLY

1. Trim the cake tops. Fill them with the swiss meringue buttercream. Frost the top and sides of the cake with the first layer (crumb coat) of buttercream and chill for 30 minutes. Once chilled, frost the top and sides of the cake with another generous layer of the buttercream and smooth using a cake scraper.

CARAMEL CAKE

Makes one three-layer 6-inch cake

This is one of my favorite cake flavor combinations with a signature cake design. Fluffy and light caramel cake layers, smooth and sweet caramel frosting, a salted caramel drip, and lots of homemade caramel popcorn make this recipe a unique addition to your collection. You can also choose to make the base cake a vanilla cake along with the caramel frosting as another option.

CARAMEL CAKE

1⅓ cups (225g) all-purpose flour

2 cups (255g) self-rising flour

1 tsp. baking powder

1½ cups (360ml) milk, at room
    temperature

1½ tsp. caramel extract

1½ cups (339g) unsalted butter,
    softened at room temperature

2½ cups (300g) sugar

2½ cups (300g) brown sugar

6 eggs

1 batch homemade caramel popcorn

CARAMEL BUTTERCREAM

1½ cups (339g) unsalted butter,
    softened at room temperature

⅓ cup (113ml) homemade (or store-
    bought) caramel sauce

1½ tsp. vanilla extract

2⅓ cups (270g) powdered sugar

pinch of salt

CARAMEL CAKE

1. Preheat the oven to 350°F (180°C).

2. Spray four 6-inch round cake pans with baking spray and line with parchment rounds.

3. Combine both flours with the baking powder and set aside.

4. Mix the milk and caramel extract and set aside.

5. In the bowl of a stand mixer fitted with the paddle attachment (or using an electric mixer), cream the butter until smooth and fluffy.

6. Scrape down the sides and add both sugars. Mix for a few minutes until very light and fluffy.

7. Add the eggs one at a time, mixing well after each addition.

8. Add the flour mixture gradually in three parts, alternating with the milk mixture and mixing well after each addition.

9. Scrape down the sides and mix again for a minute until combined.

10. Divide the cake batter evenly among the pans using a kitchen scale.

11. Bake for 25-30 minutes or until a toothpick inserted in the center of the cake comes out clean.

12. Let the cakes cool completely in the pans before flipping over onto a wire rack.

13. Wrap the cake layers in plastic wrap and chill at room temperature overnight before frosting and decorating.

CARAMEL BUTTERCREAM

1. In the bowl of a stand mixer fitted with the paddle attachment (or using an electric mixer), beat the butter for 2-3 minutes until light and fluffy.

2. Add the caramel sauce. Beat for a minute until well combined.

3. Add the vanilla and beat.

4. Scrape down the sides and add the powdered sugar all at once. Beat well for 3-4 minutes until the buttercream becomes smooth and fluffy.

5. Add a pinch of salt and mix for 30 seconds.

6. Beat the buttercream at low speed for 5 minutes to remove the air bubbles.

ASSEMBLY

1. Trim the cake tops. Fill and frost the cake layers with the caramel buttercream. Once chilled, use the caramel sauce to create a caramel drip all around the cake. If the sauce is too thick, heat it in the microwave for 5-7 seconds to loosen the consistency slightly. Top with caramel popcorn.

*NOTE: Check out the recipes for caramel sauce and caramel popcorn at the end of the book.

FRUITY PEBBLES CAKE

Makes one three-layer 6-inch cake

This cake is so much fun. Not only are the colors beautiful, but the addition of crushed Fruity Pebbles to both the cake batter and buttercream makes this cake so delicious and different.

FRUITY PEBBLES CAKE

1½ cups (170g) self-rising flour

1¼ cups (150g) all-purpose flour

1 cup (240ml) milk, at room
    temperature

1 tsp. vanilla extract

1 cup (226g) unsalted butter, softened
    for 20 minutes

2 cups (400g) granulated sugar

4 eggs, at room temperature

1 cup Fruity Pebbles cereal, crushed

FRUITY PEBBLES BUTTERCREAM

400g egg whites (12 large eggs)

3 cups (600g) sugar

3 ½ cups (800g) unsalted butter,
    softened

1 tsp. vanilla extract

¾ cup Fruity Pebbles cereal, crushed

FRUITY PEBBLES CAKE

1. Preheat the oven to 350°F (180°C). Spray three 6-inch round pans with baking spray and line the bottom with parchment rounds.

2. Combine both flours and set aside. Mix the milk and vanilla and set aside.

3. In the bowl of a stand mixer fitted with the paddle attachment (or using an electric mixer), cream the butter until smooth and fluffy.

4. Scrape down the sides and add the sugar. Beat for a few minutes until light and fluffy. Add the eggs one at a time, mixing well after each addition.

5. Add the flour mixture gradually in three parts, alternating with the milk mixture and mixing after each addition.

6. Add the crushed Fruity Pebbles cereal. Scrape down the sides and mix again for a few minutes until combined.

7. Divide the cake batter evenly among the 3 pans using a kitchen scale.

8. Bake for 25-30 minutes or until a toothpick inserted in the center of the cake comes out clean. Let the cakes cool completely in the pans before moving onto a wire rack.

9. Wrap the cake layers in plastic wrap and chill in the fridge overnight before frosting and decorating.

FRUITY PEBBLES BUTTERCREAM

1. Wipe all the tools you will be using with white vinegar or lemon juice.

2. Measure the egg whites before transferring them to a saucepan. Add the sugar and stir with a spatula.

3. Place the saucepan over medium heat and stir. Do not leave the pan while stirring. Use a candy thermometer to measure the mixture temperature. Once it reaches 150°F, take the saucepan off the heat immediately.

4. Transfer the mixture to the mixer bowl fitted with the whisk attachment and whisk it on medium/high speed until the mixture turns white and glossy and forms stiff peaks.

5. Slowly start adding the butter, a cube at a time. Keep mixing. At this point, you can switch to the paddle attachment. The mixture may turn crumbly. Keep mixing and it will eventually turn into a silky-smooth buttercream.

6. Add the vanilla extract and mix. Add the Fruity Pebbles cereal and mix at low speed for a few minutes.

ASSEMBLY

1. Trim the cake tops.

2. Fill the cake layers with the Fruity Pebbles buttercream.

3. Frost the top and sides of the cake with a thin layer of the buttercream (crumb coat) and chill for 30 minutes.

4. Cover with a final layer of the buttercream and smooth the sides using a cake scraper.

5. You can decorate the top and sides of the cake with Fruity Pebbles.

LEMON CAKE

Makes one two-layer 6-inch cake

I love everything citrusy, so this cake is a real treat for me, especially on hot summer days when it is paired with a tangy lemon buttercream. This cake boasts a citrus explosion with every bite. When I posted this cake on my social media pages as a teaser while working on the book, I received an incredible number of requests for this recipe. I had no idea that lemon cake was such a popular cake flavor! Go ahead and make this cake for that lemon-loving person in your life.

LEMON CAKE

2¼ cups (270g) cake flour*

1 Tbsp. baking powder

½ tsp. salt

4 egg whites

1¼ cups (300ml) buttermilk**

1½ cups (300g) sugar

2 tsp. lemon zest

1 cup (226g) unsalted butter, softened
    at room temperature

½ tsp. lemon extract

LEMON BUTTERCREAM

1 cup (226g) unsalted butter, softened
    at room temperature

2 Tbsp. lemon juice

2 tsp. lemon zest

2 Tbsp. milk

4½ cups (540g) powdered sugar

pinch of salt

LEMON CAKE

1. Preheat the oven to 350°F (180°C).

2. Spray two 6-inch cake pans with baking spray and line the bottom with parchment rounds.

3. In a medium-sized bowl, sift together the dry ingredients (cake flour, baking powder, and salt).

4. In another bowl, whisk the egg whites. Add the buttermilk and whisk.

5. In the bowl of a stand mixer fitted with the paddle attachment (or using an electric mixer), mix the sugar and lemon zest. Add the butter and beat until light and fluffy for about 2-3 minutes.

6. Add the lemon extract and mix just until combined.

7. Start adding the flour mixture and alternate with the buttermilk mixture until they are all added in. Mix until they are well combined.

8. Divide the batter evenly among the 3 cake pans using a kitchen scale.

9. Bake 30-35 minutes until a toothpick inserted in the center of the cake comes out clean.

LEMON BUTTERCREAM

1. In the bowl of a stand mixer fitted with the paddle attachment, beat the butter for about 3 minutes until creamy.

2. Add the lemon juice, lemon zest, and milk and mix.

3. Add the powdered sugar all at once. Mix at low speed first and then increase the speed to medium/high until the buttercream becomes fluffy and spreadable.

4. Add a small pinch of salt and mix.

5. Beat on low speed for 5 minutes to remove most of the air bubbles. Taste the buttercream. If it is too sweet, add another pinch of salt.

ASSEMBLY

1. Trim the cake tops. Fill and frost the cake layers with the lemon buttercream. Cover the top and sides of the cake with a thin layer of the buttercream (crumb coat) and chill for 30 minutes.

2. Cover the cake with another generous layer of buttercream and smooth the sides using a cake scraper. You can place the remaining buttercream in a piping bag fitted with a star piping tip (such as Wilton 1M) and use it to create a border at the top of the cake.

TIPS & TRICKS

*To make cake flour at home, measure 2½ cups flour. Remove 5 tablespoons of the flour and replace them with 5 tablespoons of corn starch. Sift and measure 2¼ cups from this mixture.

*To make buttermilk at home, add 1 tablespoon fresh lemon juice to one measuring cup.
Fill the remainder of the cup with full fat milk. Leave it for 10 minutes. This produces one cup of buttermilk.

NEAPOLITAN CAKE

Makes one three-layer 6-inch cake

Why have one cake flavor when you can have three in one slice? This is what this cake is about: layers of vanilla, chocolate, and strawberry that not only look pretty but also taste extremely delicious. In my recipe, I use my base vanilla cake recipe and flavor it into the three different flavors. I normally pair this cake with my Swiss Meringue buttercream recipe and decorate the outside of the cake with the three colors to match the three flavors inside.

NEAPOLITAN CAKE

1¼ cups + 2 Tbsp. (225g) all-purpose
  flour

1½ cups + 2 Tbsp. (255g) self-rising
  flour

1½ cups (360ml) full fat milk, at room
  temperature

1½ tsp. vanilla extract

1½ cups (339g) unsalted butter,
  softened at room temperature

3 cups (600g) sugar

6 eggs

1 tsp. strawberry extract (for the
  batter)

pink gel food coloring

1 Tbsp. cocoa powder, sifted

1 Tbsp. full fat milk

NEAPOLITAN BUTTERCREAM

1 batch Swiss meringue buttercream

¼ cup (50g) semi-sweet chocolate
  chips

½ tsp. strawberry extract

pink gel food coloring

NEAPOLITAN CAKE

1. Preheat the oven to 350°F. Spray three 6-inch pans with baking spray and line with parchment rounds.

2. Combine both flours and set aside. Mix the milk and vanilla extract and set aside.

3. In the bowl of a stand mixer fitted with the paddle attachment (or using an electric mixer), beat the butter and sugar at medium high speed for 3-4 minutes until light and fluffy.

4. Add the eggs one at a time, mixing well after each addition.

5. Add the flour mixture gradually in three parts, alternating with the milk mixture and mixing after each addition to ensure it is well combined.

6. Scrape down the sides and the bottom of the mixer bowl and mix again for a few seconds just until combined. Divide the cake batter into three bowls using a kitchen scale. Leave one of the bowls as a vanilla cake layer.

7. In the second bowl, add the strawberry extract and a few drops of the pink food coloring. Mix with a spatula until well combined. This will be the strawberry layer.

8. For the third bowl, add the cocoa powder and milk and mix until well combined. This will be the chocolate cake layer.

9. Pour each of the cake batters into a separate cake pan. Bake for 25-30 minutes or until a toothpick inserted in the center of the cake comes out clean.

10. Let the cakes cool completely in the pans before moving onto a wire rack. Wrap the cake layers in plastic wrap and chill in the fridge overnight before frosting and decorating.

NEAPOLITAN BUTTERCREAM

1. Make a batch of the Swiss meringue buttercream.

2. In a microwave-safe bowl, add the chocolate chips. Melt in the microwave in 30 second intervals. Stir after each 30 seconds. Do not overheat, as chocolate burns easily. Set aside to cool.

3. Place 250g of the buttercream in a medium-sized bowl. Add the melted chocolate and fold in using a spatula until well combined.

4. Place another 250g of the buttercream into another bowl. Add 1 teaspoon of strawberry extract and a few drops of pink gel food coloring. Fold using a spatula until well combined. Add white icing color to the remaining buttercream.

5. Now, place the three buttercream flavors into 3 piping bags: chocolate, strawberry, and plain vanilla.

ASSEMBLY

1. Trim the cake tops. Fill the cake layers with buttercream. Cover the cake with a thin layer of buttercream and chill for 30 minutes. Pipe two rounds of brown buttercream around the cake followed by two rounds of pink buttercream and finally the white buttercream as the last two rounds. Smooth the buttercream using a cake scraper.

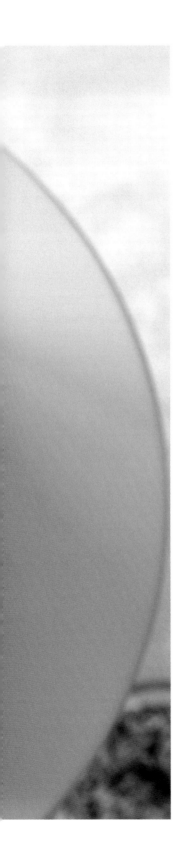

RED VELVET CONFETTI CAKE

Makes one three-layer 6-inch cake

Red velvet cake is truly one of my favorite cake flavors. For my birthday years ago, I remember my friends surprising me with a big red velvet cake covered with chocolate frosting and a pink "Happy Birthday" message on top. Since then, I set off to create the perfect homemade red velvet cake. You will love this recipe just as much as my family loves eating it every time I bake it, especially around the holiday season. For this version, I went one step further and spiced it up with a fun confetti buttercream.

RED VELVET CAKE

6 Tbsp. red liquid food coloring

1½ tsp. vanilla extract

3 Tbsp. (22g) unsweetened cocoa powder

1½ teaspoons salt

1½ cups (360ml) buttermilk*

¾ cup (185g) unsalted butter, softened at room temperature

2¼ cups (450g) sugar

3 eggs

3⅓ cups (417g) cake flour**, sifted

1½ tsp. baking soda

1½ tsp. apple cider vinegar

CONFETTI BUTTERCREAM

2 cups (454g) unsalted butter, softened

6 cups (750g) powdered sugar

4 Tbsp. (60ml) whipping cream

2 tsp. vanilla extract

½ tsp. salt

¾ cup colorful sprinkles

RED VELVET CAKE

1. Preheat the oven to 350°F (180°C). Spray three 6-inch round pans with baking spray and line with parchment rounds.

2. In a small bowl, whisk the red food coloring, vanilla extract, and cocoa powder. In a separate bowl, add the salt to the buttermilk and set aside.

3. In the bowl of a stand mixer fitted with the paddle attachment (or an electric mixer), cream the butter and sugar at medium speed for 4-5 minutes until light and fluffy.

4. Add the eggs one at a time, mixing well after each addition.

5. Add the red food coloring mixture and mix just until combined.

6. Add the buttermilk in three batches, alternating with the flour. Mix just until combined.

7. In another small bowl, mix the baking soda with the vinegar. Add to the cake batter and fold using a spatula until everything is well combined.

8. Divide the batter equally among the prepared cake pans. Bake between 35-40 minutes or until a toothpick inserted in the center comes out clean.

9. Let the cakes cool completely in the pans before flipping onto a wire rack. Cover the cakes in plastic wrap and chill in the fridge for a few hours or overnight before frosting.

CONFETTI BUTTERCREAM

1. In the bowl of a stand mixer fitted with the paddle attachment, cream the butter for 3 minutes.

2. Add the powdered sugar over 2 batches and beat for 2-3 minutes.

3. Add the whipping cream, vanilla extract, and salt.

4. Beat on high speed for 5 minutes.

5. Reduce the speed to low and beat for 5 minutes to remove the air bubbles.

6. Add the sprinkles and fold in using a spatula. Transfer to a piping bag.

ASSEMBLY

1. Trim the cake tops. Fill the cake layers with the confetti buttercream. Chill for 30 minutes. Cover the top and sides of the cake with a thin layer of the confetti buttercream. Smooth using a cake scraper. Chill for another 20- 30 minutes.

2. Once the cake has chilled, cover with a final layer of the buttercream. To decorate, you can pipe dollops of buttercream all over the cake top.

TIPS & TRICKS

*To make cake flour at home, measure 2½ cups flour. Remove 5 tablespoons of the flour and replace them with 5 tablespoons of corn starch. Sift and measure 2¼ cups from this mixture.

*To make buttermilk at home, add 1 tablespoon fresh lemon juice to one measuring cup. Fill the remainder of the cup with full fat milk. Leave it for 10 minutes. This produces one cup of buttermilk.

COOKIES & CREAM CAKE

Makes one three-layer 6-inch cake

This is a popular cake flavor. If you are looking for a cake flavor that will satisfy a large crowd (like at a birthday party), this is one of the safest options because it is loved by most people. I recently started pairing it with a cookies & cream Swiss meringue buttercream, and the result was phenomenal.

COOKIES & CREAM CAKE

3 cups (400g) flour

2½ tsp. baking powder

½ tsp. salt

1¼ cups (295ml) milk

2 tsp. vanilla extract

4 Tbsp. (54ml) canola oil

1 cup unsalted butter, softened at
    room temperature

2¼ cups sugar

5 (170g) egg whites

15 roughly crushed Oreos, cream
    removed

COOKIES & CREAM SWISS MERINGUE BUTTERCREAM

1 batch Swiss meringue buttercream

8 finely crushed Oreos, cream
    removed

1 batch chocolate ganache

COOKIES & CREAM CAKE

1. Preheat the oven to 350°F (180°C).

2. Spray three 6-inch round pans with baking spray and line with parchment rounds.

3. In a medium-sized bowl, mix the flour, baking powder, and salt and set aside.

4. In another bowl, mix the milk with the vanilla extract and oil and set aside.

5. In the bowl of a stand mixer fitted with the paddle attachment, beat the butter until smooth and creamy for about 3 minutes.

6. Add the sugar and beat for another 3 minutes until the mixture is light and fluffy.

7. Add the egg whites and mix until combined.

8. Add the dry ingredients in two batches alternating with the milk and mix just until combined.

9. Add the crushed Oreos and fold in with a spatula.

10. Divide the cake batter evenly among the prepared cake pans using a kitchen scale.

11. Bake in the preheated oven for 25-30 minutes or until a toothpick inserted in the center comes out clean.

12. Let the cakes cool in the pan for 20 minutes then invert onto a wire rack to cool completely.

13. Cover in plastic wrap and store in the fridge until ready to frost.

COOKIES & CREAM SWISS MERINGUE BUTTERCREAM

1. Make a batch of the Swiss meringue buttercream.

2. Add 8 crushed Oreos and fold in using a spatula. For a whiter cookies & cream cake, use less Oreo biscuits.

3. Transfer to a large piping bag.

ASSEMBLY

1. Trim the cake tops. Fill each cake layer with the cookies & cream Swiss meringue buttercream. Frost the cake with a thin layer of the buttercream. Chill for 30 minutes.

2. Frost the cake with a final generous layer of the buttercream and smooth the sides using a cake scraper. Chill for 20 minutes. Drip the chocolate ganache on half of the cake circumference.

3. Chill the cake and take it out 30 minutes before serving.

ALMOND CAKE

Makes one three-layer 6-inch cake

This cake is an outburst of delicious flavors in its fluffy sponge cake, creamy almond buttercream, and crunchy texture from the toasted almonds. It will leave you longing for more and more. Almond cake is must-try cake for every dessert lover.

SPONGE CAKE

5 eggs, separated into whites and yolks

¼ cup (50g) sugar for the egg whites

½ cup (100g) sugar for the egg yolks

1 tsp. vanilla extract

¾ cup (96g) flour

ALMOND BUTTERCREAM

1⅓ (300g) cups unsalted butter, softened at room temperature

1 cup dulce de leche (from a can)

1 tsp. almond extract

TOPPING

250g almond slivers

SPONGE CAKE

1. Preheat the oven to 350°F (180°C).

2. Spray three 6-inch round cake pans with baking spray and line with parchment rounds.

3. Clean the mixer bowl with white vinegar or lemon juice.

4. Whisk the egg whites until they are foamy. Start adding the sugar gradually and then beat on medium speed until the mixture doubles in volume and becomes white and glossy (meringue stage). If you lift off the whisk, a point peak appears that does not move.

5. In another bowl, whisk the egg yolks for a few minutes until they become creamy and pale in color. Add the sugar and mix.

6. Add the vanilla and mix.

7. Add the flour and mix well to combine.

8. Finally, fold in one spatula of the whipped egg whites and stir gently until combined. Add the rest of the whipped egg whites and fold in until there are no more white streaks.

9. Divide the cake batter evenly among the cake pans.

10. Bake for about 20 minutes or until a toothpick inserted in the center comes out clean.

11. Let cool in the pans for 15 minutes then flip over a wire rack to cool completely. Cover in plastic wrap and store at room temperature for a few hours.

ALMOND BUTTERCREAM

1. In the bowl of a stand mixer fitted with the paddle attachment, beat the butter for 3-5 minutes until light and creamy.

2. Add the dulce de leche and mix.

3. Add the almond extract and mix.

4. Beat at high speed for 2 minutes then reduce the speed to low and beat for 5 minutes.

TOPPING

1. Toast the almonds in a baking sheet in a pre-heated oven at 160°C for 5 minutes until golden in color.

ASSEMBLY

1. Trim the cake tops. Fill and frost with the almond buttercream. Chill the frosted cake for 15 minutes.

2. Place the chilled cake on a cake turntable. Use your hands to stick the toasted almonds all over the sides and top of the cake. Store the cake in the fridge until ready to serve.

CHOCOLATE YELLOW CAKE

Makes one three-layer 6-inch cake

I have always been tempted to grab the yellow cake mixes from the grocery store, so I set out to create a yellow cake from scratch at home. For this cake, I used not only eggs, but also extra egg yolks to give the cake a natural yellow color. In addition, I used both butter and canola oil to give it that extra moisture. I paired this cake with the perfect chocolate frosting.

YELLOW CAKE

2½ cups (300g) cake flour*

2 tsp. baking powder

½ tsp. salt

½ cup (113g) unsalted butter, softened

1¼ cups (250g) sugar

¼ cup (60ml) canola oil

1½ tsp. vanilla extract

3 eggs

2 egg yolks

1 cup (240ml) buttermilk

CHOCOLATE FROSTING

1 batch of chocolate frosting, see
    recipe on page 156

YELLOW CAKE

1. Preheat the oven to 350°F (180°C).

2. Spray three 6-inch cake pans with baking spray and line with parchment rounds.

3. In a medium bowl, mix the dry ingredients (cake flour, baking powder, and salt).

4. In the bowl of a stand mixer fitted with the paddle attachment or using an electric mixer, beat the butter until creamy and smooth for 2 minutes. Add the sugar and beat for 2-3 minutes.

5. Add the oil and mix until combined.

6. Add the vanilla extract and mix.

7. Add the eggs and egg yolks one at a time mixing well after each addition.

8. Add a third of the flour mixture, alternating with the buttermilk mixture and mixing after each addition until all the ingredients are added in.

9. Divide the cake batter evenly among the prepared pans.

10. Bake for 25-30 minutes or until a toothpick inserted in the center comes out clean.

11. Let the cakes cool in the pans for 10 minutes before inverting on a wire rack to cool completely.

12. Wrap in plastic wrap and store at room temperature or in the fridge overnight before frosting and decorating.

ASSEMBLY

1. Trim the cake tops.

2. Make a batch of chocolate frosting. See page 156.

3. Fill and frost the cake with a thin layer of the chocolate frosting. Chill for 30 minutes.

4. Cover with a final generous layer of the chocolate frosting.

TIPS & TRICKS

*To make cake flour at home, measure 2½ cups flour. Remove 5 tablespoons of the flour and replace them with 5 tablespoons of corn starch. Sift and measure 2¼ cups from this mixture.

*To make buttermilk at home, add 1 tablespoon fresh lemon juice to one measuring cup. Fill the remainder of the cup with full fat milk. Leave it for 10 minutes. This produces one cup of buttermilk.

BLACK FOREST CAKE

Makes one three-layer 6-inch cake

While I was growing up, Black Forest cake was the cake my parents always bought us for birthdays and important events. Fast forward years later, I bake almost every single day, and never once did I think about baking a Black Forest cake until I came across a picture on social media which brought back all my happy childhood memories. This is one of the cakes that I simply cannot resist.

CHOCOLATE GENOISE

⅔ cup (80g) flour

½ cup (45g) unsweetened cocoa
  powder

5 eggs

½ cup + 2 Tbsp. (125g) sugar

CHANTILLY CREAM

2 ½ cups (600ml) whipping cream

½ cup (60g) powdered sugar

1 tsp. vanilla extract

CAKE ASSEMBLY

1 (15oz.) (420g) mixed fruit can (or
  maraschino cherries) & syrup

chocolate sprinkles (or curls)

CHOCOLATE GENOISE

1. Preheat the oven to 350°F (180°C).

2. Spray three 6-inch cake pans with baking spray and line with parchment rounds.

3. In a small bowl, sift the flour and cocoa powder and set aside.

4. In the bowl of a stand mixer fitted with the whisk attachment, beat the eggs and sugar for 5-6 minutes until the mixture triples in volume and becomes lighter in color. If you lift the whisk up, the batter should fall off to form a thick, glossy, light yellow ribbon.

5. Add the flour mixture and fold it in very gently with a spatula until combined so the egg mixture does not deflate.

6. Pour into the prepared cake pans and bake in the preheated oven for 20-25 minutes or until a toothpick inserted in the center comes out almost clean.

7. Let the cakes cool in the pans for 10 minutes before inverting on a wire rack to cool completely.

8. Wrap in plastic wrap and store at room temperature for a few hours before frosting and decorating.

CHANTILLY CREAM

1. In the bowl of a stand mixer fitted with the whisk attachment, mix the whipping cream for 5 minutes until it thickens and becomes glossy. Add the powdered sugar and vanilla and beat for another 30 seconds. The Chantilly cream can be made in advance and stored in the fridge until cake assembly.

ASSEMBLY

1. Trim the cake tops. Soak each cake layer with the syrup of the fruit.

2. Fill the cake with the Chantilly cream followed by the fruit. Cover the fruits with more cream and top with another cake layer and repeat until you have stacked the three layers.

3. Frost the outside of the cake with a thin layer of the Chantilly cream and chill for 30 minutes. Frost with another layer of the Chantilly cream. Chill for another 30 minutes.

4. Cover the entire sides and top of the frosted cake with the chocolate sprinkles.

PEANUT BUTTER & CHOCOLATE CAKE

Makes one three-layer 6-inch cake

I love peanut butter, whether it's with breakfast or just a snack, and I often add it in my dessert recipes. This cake is dedicated to all the peanut butter lovers out there. Chocolate cake layers filled with smooth peanut butter frosting and a glossy chocolate ganache drip makes this one a dream.

TIPS & TRICKS

* To make buttermilk at home, add 1 tablespoon fresh lemon juice to one measuring cup.
Fill the remainder of the cup with full fat milk. Leave it for 10 minutes. This produces one cup of buttermilk.

CHOCOLATE CAKE

2¼ cups (285g) flour

2¼ cups (450g) sugar

1 cup (120g) unsweetened cocoa
   powder

1½ tsp. baking powder

1 Tbsp. baking soda

1 tsp. salt

1½ cups (360ml) buttermilk*

1 cup (240ml) coffee

¾ cup (180ml) canola oil

3 eggs

2 tsp. vanilla extract

PEANUT BUTTER FROSTING

1½ cups (339g) unsalted butter,
   softened at room temperature

1½ cups (360g) creamy peanut butter

1½ tsp. vanilla extract

pinch of salt

3 cups (285g) powdered sugar

2 Tbsp. full fat milk

TOPPING

½ cup chocolate frosting (optional)

CHOCOLATE CAKE

1. Preheat the oven to 350°F (180°C).

2. Spray three 6-inch pans with baking spray and line with parchment rounds.

3. First, measure the dry ingredients (flour, sugar, cocoa powder, baking powder, baking soda, and salt) and sift them into the bowl of a stand mixer or a medium-sized bowl.

4. In a separate bowl, measure the wet ingredients (buttermilk, coffee, and canola oil). Then add the eggs one by one, whisking well after each addition. Add the vanilla extract.

5. Add the wet ingredients to the dry ingredients. Using the paddle attachment of the stand mixer, mix them just until combined.

6. Stop the mixer. Scrape down the sides and the bottom of the mixer bowl. Mix again for a few seconds just until combined.

7. Divide the batter evenly among the prepared baking pans using a kitchen scale.

8. Bake 20-25 minutes or just until a toothpick inserted in the center comes out clean.

9. Let the cakes cool for half an hour in the cake pans before inverting onto a wire rack to cool completely.

10. Wrap the cake layers in plastic wrap and chill in the fridge overnight before frosting and decorating.

PEANUT BUTTER FROSTING

1. In the bowl of a stand mixer fitted with the paddle attachment, beat the butter for 30 seconds until light and fluffy.

2. Add the peanut butter and beat until well combined and creamy for 2-3 minutes.

3. Add the vanilla extract and salt and mix until combined.

4. Add the powdered sugar all at once and mix on low speed until combined.

5. Add the milk and beat at medium/high speed for a few minutes. Then reduce the speed to low and beat for 5 minutes.

ASSEMBLY

1. Trim the cake tops. Fill the cake with the peanut butter frosting. Cover with a thin layer of the frosting. Chill for 30 minutes.

2. To create the peanut butter and chocolate marble effect, pipe swirls of peanut butter frosting around most of the cake sides, leaving some random spots empty for the chocolate frosting. Then pipe random swirls of chocolate on the empty spots. Scrape the cake to create the marble effect. If there are gaps, fill them with either chocolate or peanut butter frosting and keep scraping until the cake sides are smooth. You can also cover the cake with just peanut butter frosting.

CHOCOLATE ORANGE CAKE

Makes one three-layer 6-inch cake

I was inspired to make this cake while passing by the chocolate cake aisle at the grocery store and I saw the different dark chocolate combinations. I remembered one of my friends who lives in Dubai asking me one summer to grab him a couple of chocolate and orange bars while I was visiting Lebanon since he could no longer find these bars in Dubai. As a result of this inspiring memory, I thought this cake combination would turn out delicious, and I was not disappointed.

CHOCOLATE ORANGE CAKE

2¼ cups (285g) flour

2¼ cups (450g) sugar

1 cup (120g) unsweetened cocoa powder

1½ tsp. baking powder

1 Tbsp. baking soda

1 tsp. salt

1½ cups (360ml) buttermilk

1 cup (240ml) orange juice

¾ cup (180ml) canola oil

3 eggs, at room temperature

2 tsp. vanilla extract

ORANGE BUTTERCREAM

1½ cups (339g) unsalted butter, softened
    at room temperature

zest of 2 oranges

6 cups (750g) powdered sugar

1 tsp. vanilla extract

¼ cup (60ml) orange juice

orange food gel color (optional)

CANDIED ORANGES (OPTIONAL)

¾ cup (400ml) water

2 cups (400g) sugar

4-5 fresh orange slices

CHOCOLATE ORANGE CAKE

1. Preheat the oven to 350°F (180°C).

2. Spray three 6-inch pans with baking spray and line with parchment rounds.

3. Measure the dry ingredients (flour, sugar, cocoa powder, baking powder, baking soda, and salt) and sift them into the stand mixer bowl.

4. In a separate bowl, weigh the wet ingredients (buttermilk, orange juice, and oil). Then add the eggs one by one, whisking well after each addition. Add the vanilla extract.

5. Add the wet ingredients to the dry ingredients. Using the paddle attachment of the stand mixer, mix them just until combined.

6. Stop the mixer. Scrape down the sides and the bottom of the mixer bowl. Mix again for a few seconds just until combined.

7. Divide the batter evenly among the prepared baking pans using a kitchen scale.

8. Bake 20-25 minutes or just until a toothpick inserted comes out clean.

9. Let the cakes cool in the cake pans before inverting onto a wire rack.

10. Wrap the cake layers in plastic wrap and chill in the fridge overnight before frosting and decorating.

ORANGE BUTTERCREAM

1. In the bowl of a stand mixer fitted with the paddle attachment, beat the butter with the orange zest for a few minutes until light and fluffy.

2. Add the powdered sugar and beat very well for 5-10 minutes until the buttercream is fluffy and smooth.

3. Add the vanilla extract and orange juice and mix until combined.

4. Reduce the speed to low and beat for 5 minutes to remove air bubbles.

CANDIED ORANGES

1. Place the water and sugar in a medium saucepan over medium heat.

2. Stir until the sugar dissolves and the mixture boils.

3. Once the mixture boils, place the orange slices in it carefully, one by one, and let the mixture simmer over low heat without stirring for 30 minutes.

4. Take the mixture off the heat and let the orange slices cool in the syrup.

5. Use tongs to transfer the orange slices to a wire rack placed over a baking sheet and let them cool completely.

ASSEMBLY

1. Trim the cake tops.

2. Fill and frost with a thin layer of the orange buttercream.

3. Chill for 30 minutes.

4. Frost the cake with a final layer of the buttercream. Smooth the cake sides using a cake scraper. Decorate with the candied oranges on top.

PUMPKIN SPICE CAKE

Makes one three-layer 6-inch cake

Fall is my favorite season of the year. Although we don't get a proper fall in Dubai until the end of October, I get myself in the fall mood starting in September by decorating the house with pumpkins and Halloween decorations. I start baking all sorts of pumpkin spice bakes, even making pumpkin spice lattes at home. I just love the fall vibes, and this cake is one of my favorite cakes to make during the season! If you are anything like me, you have to add this to your fall baking list.

PUMPKIN SPICE CAKE

2 cups (250g) flour

2 tsp. baking powder

1 tsp. baking soda

2 tsp. ground cinnamon

½ tsp. ground ginger

½ tsp. ground nutmeg

¼ tsp. ground cloves

½ tsp. salt

1 cup (200g) light brown sugar

½ cup (100g) sugar

2 cups (500g) pumpkin puree

1 cup (240ml) canola oil

2 tsp. vanilla extract

4 eggs

CREAM CHEESE FROSTING

½ cup (113g) unsalted butter, softened
    at room temperature

1 cup (226g) cream cheese, softened at
    room temperature

1 tsp. vanilla extract

¼ tsp. salt

4 cups (500g) powdered sugar

PUMPKIN SPICE CAKE

1. Preheat the oven to 350°F (180°C).

2. Spray three 6-inch cake pans with baking spray and line with parchment rounds.

3. In a medium-sized bowl, measure the flour, baking powder, baking soda, cinnamon, ginger, nutmeg, cloves, and salt and set aside.

4. In the bowl of a stand mixer fitted with the paddle attachment (or using an electric mixer), beat both sugars with the pumpkin puree, oil, and vanilla extract for 3 minutes until the mixture is smooth.

5. Add the eggs one at a time and beat until smooth.

6. Add the flour mixture in two parts and beat just until combined.

7. Divide the cake batter evenly into the prepared pans using a kitchen scale.

8. Bake for 25-27 minutes or until a toothpick inserted in the center of the cake comes out clean.

9. Let cool in the pan for 10 minutes, and then invert onto a wire rack to cool completely.

10. Cover with plastic wrap and refrigerate overnight before frosting and decorating.

CREAM CHEESE FROSTING

1. In the bowl of a stand mixer fitted with the paddle attachment, beat the butter and cream cheese for 2-3 minutes until smooth.

2. Add the vanilla extract and salt and beat for another 2 minutes.

3. Add the powdered sugar gradually and beat at high speed for 5 minutes until the frosting is smooth and creamy.

4. Reduce the speed to low and beat for 5 minutes to remove the air bubbles.

ASSEMBLY

1. Trim the cake tops. Fill and frost with the cream cheese frosting. Smooth the sides of the cake using a cake scraper.

2. You can color a bit of the leftover cream cheese frosting with orange gel food color and use a French star tip to pipe small pumpkins on top of the cake.

TRIPLE CHOCOLATE CAKE

Makes one three-layer 6-inch cake

I first set out to make this cake as a fun cake design, but when I saw how everyone reacted after posting the cake on my social media pages, I knew that the recipe had to make it in the book. It is a fun cake with three delicious layers: chocolate, caramel, and vanilla. This cake is decorated with an ombre brown rosette buttercream design on the outside—so simple, yet so impressive.

CHOCOLATE CAKE LAYER

1¾ cups (225g) flour

2¼ Tbsp. (17g) unsweetened cocoa
    powder

1 tsp. baking powder

½ Tbsp. baking soda

¼ tsp. salt

½ cup (100g) semi-sweet chocolate
    chips

½ cup + 2 Tbsp. (150ml) full fat milk

1¾ cups (340g) brown sugar

½ cup (100g) unsalted butter

3 eggs

CARAMEL CAKE LAYER

¼ cup (55g) unsalted butter

½ cup + 1 Tbsp. (125g) sugar

¼ cup + 2 Tbsp. (75g) brown sugar

2 tsp. vanilla extract

2 eggs

1 cup (140g) flour

½ cup (120ml) buttermilk

½ tsp. baking soda

½ Tbsp. (7g) white vinegar

VANILLA CAKE LAYER

½ cup + 2 Tbsp. (100g) self-rising
    flour

pinch of salt

½ cup (100g) unsalted butter

½ cup (100g) sugar

1 tsp. vanilla extract

2 eggs

MILK SOAK

½ cup (100ml) full fat milk

2 tsp. vanilla extract

TRIPLE CHOCOLATE BUTTERCREAM

2 cups (454g) unsalted butter,
    softened

5 cups (560g) powdered sugar

1 tsp. vanilla extract

ivory and brown gel food colors

DIRECTIONS

1. Preheat the oven to 340°F.

2. Spray three 6-inch cake pans with baking spray and line with parchment rounds.

CHOCOLATE CAKE LAYER

1. In a medium bowl, mix the flour, cocoa powder, baking powder, baking soda, and salt. Set aside.

2. In a medium saucepan, place the chocolate chips, milk, and half of the brown sugar over medium heat. Bring to a boil.

3. In the bowl of a stand mixer fitted with the paddle attachment, beat the butter and the remaining brown sugar until light and fluffy for about 5 minutes.

4. Add the eggs one at a time, mixing well after each addition.

5. Add the flour mixture and beat just until combined.

6. Add the chocolate mixture and beat at low speed just until combined.

7. Pour the chocolate cake batter into one of the prepared cake pans.

8. Bake for 30 minutes or until a toothpick inserted in the center comes out almost clean.

9. Let the cake cool in the pan for 10 minutes before inverting onto a wire rack.

10. Cover the cooled cake with plastic wrap and leave it at room temperature overnight before decorating.

CARAMEL CAKE LAYER

1. In the bowl of a stand mixer fitted with the paddle attachment (or using an electric mixer), beat the butter and both sugars for about 5 minutes until light and fluffy.

2. Add the vanilla extract and beat for a few seconds.

3. Add the eggs one at a time, mixing well after each addition.

4. Add the flour and buttermilk and beat just until combined.

5. In a small bowl, mix the baking soda and vinegar and fold it quickly into the prepared cake batter.

6. Pour the caramel cake batter into one of the prepared cake pans.

7. Bake for 30 minutes or until a toothpick inserted in the center comes out clean.

8. Let the cake cool in the pan for 10 minutes before inverting onto a wire rack.

9. Cover the cooled cake with plastic wrap and leave it at room temperature overnight before decorating.

VANILLA CAKE LAYER

1. In a medium-sized bowl, mix the flour and salt and set aside.

2. In the bowl of a stand mixer fitted with the paddle attachment, beat the butter and sugar until light and fluffy for about 5 minutes.

3. Add the vanilla extract and beat for a few seconds.

4. Add the eggs one at a time, mixing well after each addition.

5. Add the flour mixture and beat just until combined.

6. Pour the cake batter into one of the prepared cake pans.

7. Bake for 25 minutes or until a toothpick inserted in the center comes out clean.

8. Let the cake cool in the pan for 10 minutes before inverting onto a wire rack.

9. Cover the cooled cake with plastic wrap and leave it at room temperature overnight before decorating.

10. Whisk the milk soak ingredients in a small bowl and set aside for cake assembly.

TRIPLE CHOCOLATE BUTTERCREAM

1. In the bowl of a stand mixer fitted with the paddle attachment, beat the butter at high speed for about 5 minutes until light and fluffy.

2. Add the powdered sugar all at once and beat at low speed until well combined. Then beat at high speed for a minute.

3. Add the vanilla extract and beat for 30 seconds at low speed.

4. Increase the speed to high and beat for at least 5 minutes. Then reduce the speed to the lowest setting and beat for 5 minutes. This will help reduce the air bubbles.

5. Split the buttercream into 3 bowls equally.

6. Add one drop of ivory food color to one of the bowls. Using a spatula, fold in until well combined.

7. Add 4-5 drops of the same ivory food color to the next bowl and brown food color to the third bowl. Fold the color into each bowl until well combined.

8. Leave some of the buttercream aside for the cake filling and crumb coat. Prepare 3 piping bags, each fitted with the Wilton 1M (or any star) piping tip. Scoop each buttercream color into a piping bag.

ASSEMBLY

1. Once ready to decorate, trim the cake tops and start layering them on a cake board. Soak each cake layer with the milk soak using a pastry brush then pipe buttercream for the filling. Cover the cake with a thin layer of buttercream as the crumb coat and chill for 30 minutes.

2. To decorate the cake, pipe rosettes in alternating colors. To pipe a rosette, place the piping tip perpendicular to the cake and start piping a rosette from the center and going anti-clockwise. Alternate each rosette with a different buttercream color to get the ombre effect. Make sure the rosette tops are always aligned for each line. Chill until ready to serve.

VICTORIA SPONGE CAKE

Makes one two-layer 6-inch cake

This is a beautiful rustic and effortless cake that is as pretty as it is delicious. It is perfect if you want to make a simple cake for an event at home. It makes the perfect centerpiece for any special occasion, from an afternoon tea party with friends to even an outdoor garden event.

SPONGE CAKE

1¼ cups (166g) flour

3¼ tsp. baking powder

1 tsp. salt

¾ cup (170g) unsalted butter

¾ cup (175g) sugar

1 tsp. vanilla extract

3 eggs

2 Tbsp. full fat milk

FILLING

1 cup (240ml) whipping cream

1 Tbsp. powdered sugar

¼ teaspoon vanilla extract

½ cup strawberry jam

fresh strawberries

edible flowers (optional)

SPONGE CAKE

1. Preheat the oven to 350°F (180°C).
2. Spray two 6-inch cake pans with baking spray and line with parchment rounds.
3. In a medium-sized bowl, whisk the flour, baking powder, and salt. Set aside.
4. In the bowl of a stand mixer fitted with the paddle attachment, beat the butter and sugar for about 5 minutes until light and fluffy.
5. Add the vanilla and beat for 30 seconds.
6. Add the eggs one at a time, mixing well after each addition.
7. Add the milk and mix until combined.
8. Add the flour mixture and mix just until combined.
9. Divide the batter evenly among the two prepared pans.
10. Bake 20-22 minutes or until a toothpick inserted in the center of the cake comes out almost clean.
11. Let the cakes cool in the pan for 15 minutes then invert onto a wire rack to cool completely. Cover in plastic wrap and set aside until you prepare the filling.

FILLING

1. Using an electric mixer, whisk the whipping cream, powdered sugar, and vanilla until you reach almost stiff peaks.

ASSEMBLY

1. Trim the sponge cake tops. To assemble the cake, place one layer of the cake at the bottom.
2. Spread strawberry jam all over the top of the cake layer. Spread half of the whipped cream. Top with sliced strawberries. Then, place the second layer (flat part to the top) over the first cake layer. Spread some of the remaining whipped cream in the center and top with the whole strawberries and edible flowers if using.
3. Dust the cake top and strawberries with powdered sugar.

COCONUT CUSTARD CAKE

Makes one two-layer 8-inch cake

The idea for this cake actually came from a poll I posted on my Instagram account where I had asked friends to share cake flavor ideas. As soon as I saw the word "coconut," I knew that it was the one I wanted to add in the book. I also wanted the filling to be unique, so I thought about trying out a custard filling. I had seen videos where creamy custard was being used as a cake filling, and I thought it was such a cool and delicious idea. I usually decorate the cake with vanilla buttercream and cover it all over with toasted coconut.

COCONUT CAKE

5 egg whites

2½ cups (325g) cake flour*

1 Tbsp. baking powder

½ tsp. salt

¾ cup (180ml) buttermilk**

¾ cup (185g) butter, softened

1¾ cups (350g) sugar

1 tsp. vanilla extract

½ tsp. almond extract

1 cup (77g) coconut powder

1 batch vanilla buttercream

CUSTARD FILLING

400g homemade custard

¾ cup whipping cream

TOPPING

2 cups desiccated coconut, toasted

COCONUT CAKE

1. Separate the egg whites while they are cold and leave them at room temperature for 30 minutes.

2. Mix the flour, baking powder, and salt and set aside.

3. Combine ¼ cup of the buttermilk with the egg whites and set aside.

4. In the bowl of a stand mixer fitted with the paddle attachment, beat the butter and sugar for 3-4 minutes until light and fluffy.

5. Add the vanilla and mix until combined.

6. Add the egg whites and beat for another 3 minutes.

7. Add the remaining buttermilk and mix.

8. Finally, add the cake flour mixture and mix just until combined.

9. Divide the cake batter evenly among the prepared cake pans.

10. Bake 26-28 minutes until a toothpick inserted in the center comes out almost clean.

11. Let the cakes cool in the cake pan for 5 minutes. Then invert into a wire rack and wrap in plastic wrap while hot to maintain moisture. Store in the fridge overnight or for a few hours before filling.

CUSTARD FILLING

1. Make a batch of the homemade custard.

2. Measure 400g in a bowl.

3. Whip the whipping cream for 5 minutes until you get stiff peaks.

4. Fold the whipping cream into the custard gently until you no longer see white streaks.

5. Cover and set in the fridge for a few hours or overnight.

ASSEMBLY

1. To assemble the cake, trim the cake tops using a serrated knife. Pipe a rim of vanilla buttercream around the edges of each cake layer. Fill with the custard filling. The buttercream will prevent the soft filling from going outside.

2. Repeat with the remaining layers. Cover the cake with the buttercream and smooth the sides. Let it chill and then cover the entire cake with the toasted coconut.

TIPS & TRICKS

*To make cake flour at home, measure 2½ cups flour. Remove 5 tablespoons of the flour and replace them with 5 tablespoons of corn starch. Sift and measure 2¼ cups from this mixture.

* To make buttermilk at home, add 1 tablespoon fresh lemon juice to one measuring cup.
Fill the remainder of the cup with full fat milk. Leave it for 10 minutes. This produces one cup of buttermilk.

VANILLA & BLACKBERRY COMPOTE CAKE

Makes one three-layer 6-inch cake

Berries are an excellent addition to many cake flavors, especially vanilla. You can layer in jam as a filling between cake layers or you can choose to make a homemade berry compote yourself, which will result in a rich and delicious cake perfect for a spring or summer day.

VANILLA CAKE

1 batch baked vanilla cake, see recipe
    on page 12

SWISS MERINGUE
BUTTERCREAM

1 batch Swiss meringue buttercream,
    see recipe on page 155

BLACKBERRY COMPOTE

2 cups fresh blackberries, rinsed and
    dried

1 tsp. lemon juice

¼ cup (50g) sugar

pinch of salt

TOPPING

fresh berries and mint leaves for
    decoration

VANILLA CAKE

1. Prepare the vanilla cake as directed in the vanilla cake recipe
   on page 12.

SWISS MERINGUE BUTTERCREAM

1. Prepare the Swiss meringue buttercream as directed on page
   155.

BLACKBERRY COMPOTE

1. To prepare the berry compote, place the washed and dried
   blackberries, lemon juice, sugar, and salt in a medium saucepan.
   Stir and set aside for 5 minutes.

2. Heat until the mixture boils. Let it boil for 5 minutes.

3. Reduce the heat and simmer for 10-15 minutes until the
   compote has thickened slightly. To speed up the process, you
   can mash the blackberries that did not melt.

4. Place into a jar and cool before filling the cake. It may be stored
   in the fridge.

ASSEMBLY

1. To assemble the cake, trim the vanilla cake tops. Spread a thin layer of buttercream on each cake layer and pipe
   a rim around the edges.

2. Place about a ¼ cup of the homemade blackberry compote between each layer. Top with another cake layer and
   repeat the process.

3. Cover the cake with the vanilla buttercream. Smooth the cake top and sides. You can decorate with some fresh
   berries and mint leaves.

STRAWBERRY SHORTCAKE

Makes one three-layer 8-inch cake

This is a delicious, fresh cake made for hot days. The cake is light and fluffy, and the Chantilly cream filling is always a crowd favorite. Strawberry shortcake is a must-try on anyone's baking list.

SHORTCAKE

2¼ cups (270g) cake flour*

1½ cups (300g) sugar

½ tsp. salt

2¼ tsp. baking powder

½ cup (108ml) canola oil

7 eggs, separated into yolks and whites

¾ cup (177ml) milk

2 tsp. vanilla extract

½ tsp. cream of tartar

FRESH BERRIES

about 8 cups fresh strawberries,
    quartered

½ cup (100g) sugar

1 Tbsp. lemon juice

pinch of salt

CHANTILLY CREAM

2 cups (480ml) whipping cream

¼ cup (32g) powdered sugar

SHORTCAKE

1. Preheat the oven to 325°F (160°C).

2. Spray three 8-inch round cake pans with baking spray and line with parchment rounds.

3. In a medium bowl, mix the cake flour, sugar, salt, and baking powder and set aside.

4. In another bowl, mix the oil, 7 egg yolks, and milk. Add the flour mixture and mix until combined.

5. Wipe the bowl of a stand mixer and the whisk attachment with white vinegar. Then beat the 7 egg whites until bubbles appear at the surface. Add the vanilla extract and cream of tartar and whisk at high speed until you get stiff glossy peaks. If you lift the whisk up, a pointy peak that does not wiggle appears.

6. Take a third of the egg white mixture and fold it into the prepared cake batter. Gently fold in the remaining egg white mixture until no white streaks appear.

7. Divide the cake batter into the prepared cake pans and bake for about 55 minutes until the top of the cake springs back when touched.

8. Invert the pans over a wire rack and let the cakes cool in the pan for one hour.

FRESH BERRIES

1. In a large bowl, mix the cut strawberries, sugar, lemon juice, and salt and let them sit for one hour while the cakes are cooling.

CHANTILLY CREAM

1. In the bowl of a stand mixer fitted with the whisk attachment (or using an electric mixer), beat the cream and powdered sugar for 5-7 minutes until medium glossy peaks appear.

ASSEMBLY

1. Trim the cake tops. Place a cake layer then top with half of the marinated berries. Top with the whipped Chantilly cream. Add a cake layer, then repeat by topping with the other half of the marinated berries and whipped Chantilly cream and finish it off with the final cake layer.

2. This cake is best served as a naked cake. Refrigerate for one hour.

TIPS & TRICKS

*To make cake flour at home, measure 2½ cups flour. Remove 5 tablespoons of the flour and replace them with 5 tablespoons of corn starch. Sift and measure 2¼ cups from this mixture.

BOSTON CREAM PIE CAKE

Makes one two-layer 8-inch cake

The Boston cream donut has been my husband's favorite donut since we were teenagers, so I wanted to surprise him with it in cake form. I opted for a vanilla cake base and pastry cream as the filling. Drizzle my glossy chocolate ganache on top, and the result will be a heavenly treat.

BOSTON CREAM PIE CAKE

1½ cups (170g) self-rising flour

1¼ cups (150g) all-purpose flour

1 cup full fat milk

1 tsp. vanilla extract

1 cup (226g) unsalted butter, softened

2 cups (400g) sugar

4 eggs

PASTRY CREAM

1 batch of pastry cream, see recipe on page 162

CHOCOLATE GANACHE

1 batch of chocolate ganache, see recipe on page 157

BOSTON CREAM PIE CAKE

1. Preheat the oven to 350°F (180°C).
2. Spray two 8-inch pans round pans with baking spray and line with parchment rounds.
3. Combine both flours and set aside.
4. Mix the milk and vanilla extract and set aside.
5. In the bowl of a stand mixer fitted with the paddle attachment (or using an electric mixer), cream the butter until smooth and fluffy for about 3 minutes.
6. Scrape down the sides, add the sugar, and beat for 2-3 more minutes.
7. Add the eggs one at a time, mixing well after each addition.
8. Add the flour mixture gradually in three parts alternating with the milk and vanilla mixing after each addition to ensure well combined.
9. Scrape down the sides and the bottom of the mixer bowl and mix again for a few seconds just until combined.
10. Divide the cake batter evenly among the two prepared pans using a kitchen scale.
11. Bake for 25-30 minutes or until a toothpick inserted in the center of the cake comes out clean.
12. Let the cakes cool completely in the pans before inverting onto a wire rack.
13. Wrap the cake layers in plastic wrap and chill in the fridge for a few hours before trimming and filling.

PASTRY CREAM

1. Make a batch of pastry cream (can be made the night before). See page 162.

ASSEMBLY

1. Scoop the pastry cream into a piping bag. Once the cake has chilled, trim the tops using a serrated knife.
2. Place the first layer on a cake board. Fill with the pastry cream. Cover with the other cake layer (bottom side up). Chill the cake for 30 minutes.
3. While the cake is chilling, make a fresh batch of chocolate ganache. See page 157. Let the chocolate ganache cool slightly until it reaches a dripping consistency. Drip the ganache over the chilled cake. If you want a thicker drip, let the ganache set for a longer time until you reach your desired consistency.
4. Chill the cake and take out at least 30 minutes before serving.

CARROT CAKE

Makes one three-layer 8-inch cake

Carrot cake reminds me of my early days as a banker. One of my colleagues used to bring her "special" carrot cake paired with cream cheese frosting, and everyone at the office would fall for it head over heels; as always, beautiful memories were created over a delicious cake. The cake is naturally moist from the grated carrots and makes for the perfect breakfast or snack along with a cup of hot coffee or tea.

CARROT CAKE

2 cups (250g) flour

2 tsp. baking powder

2 tsp. baking soda

2 tsp. cinnamon

½ tsp. salt

3 cups (300g) grated carrots

1 cup (100g) chopped walnuts

1 cup (80g) desiccated coconut

½ cup (65g) raisins

2 cups (400g) sugar

1 cup (210ml) canola oil

4 eggs

½ tsp. vanilla extract

CREAM CHEESE FROSTING

½ cup (113g) unsalted butter, softened

1 cup (226g) cream cheese, softened

1 tsp. vanilla extract

¼ tsp. salt

4 cups (500g) powdered sugar

CARROT CAKE

1. Preheat the oven to 325°F.

2. Spray three 8-inch pans round pans with baking spray and line with parchment rounds.

3. In a medium bowl, mix the flour, baking powder, baking soda, cinnamon, and salt and set aside.

4. In another bowl, mix the carrots, walnuts, coconut, and raisins.

5. In the bowl of a stand mixer fitted with the paddle attachment (or using an electric mixer), beat the sugar and oil for 3 minutes until smooth.

6. Add the eggs one at a time, mixing well after each addition.

7. Add the vanilla and mix.

8. Reduce the speed to low and add the flour mixture in two batches. Beat just until combined.

9. Add the carrot mixture and beat at low speed just until combined.

10. Divide the batter into the prepared pans using a kitchen scale.

11. Bake for 40-50 minutes or until a toothpick inserted in the center comes out clean.

12. Let the cakes cool in the pans for 5 minutes before inverting onto a wire rack to cool slightly.

13. Cover in plastic wrap and store in the fridge overnight.

CREAM CHEESE FROSTING

1. In the bowl of a stand mixer fitted with the paddle attachment, beat the butter and cream cheese for 2-3 minutes until smooth.

2. Add the vanilla extract and salt and beat for another 2 minutes.

3. Add the powdered sugar gradually and beat at high speed for 5 minutes until the frosting is smooth and creamy.

4. Reduce the speed to low and beat for 5 minutes to remove the air bubbles.

5. Place the frosting in the fridge for a maximum of 5 minutes before frosting the cake.

ASSEMBLY

1. Trim the cake tops. Fill the cake layers with the cream cheese frosting. Chill for 30 minutes before icing the outside of the cake.

2. Then cover the cake with a thin layer of the cream cheese frosting to create a semi-naked effect.

3. Top with fondant carrot shapes if desired.

ICE CREAM BIRTHDAY CAKE

Makes one two-layer 7-inch cake

Cake and ice cream in one, this cake will surely be the hit of any party you make it for. With a layer of chocolate ice cream, a filling of chocolate ganache and Oreo crumbs, and a final layer of vanilla ice cream, this cake is what dessert dreams are made of.

ICE CREAM BIRTHDAY CAKE

1 box (1 quart) chocolate ice cream

1 box (1 quart) vanilla ice cream

9 Oreos, crushed

1 ½ Tbsp. unsalted butter, melted

CHOCOLATE GANACHE FILLING

1 cup (167g) semi-sweet chocolate
   chips

3 Tbsp. light corn syrup

½ cup (120ml) whipping creams

TOPPING

Confetti sprinkles

ICE CREAM BIRTHDAY CAKE

1. Line a deep 7-inch cake pan with plastic wrap that goes all over the sides.

2. Preheat the oven to 350°F (180°C).

3. Line a baking sheet with parchment paper.

4. In a small bowl, pour the melted butter over the crushed Oreos and mix.

5. Spread the crushed Oreos in the prepared baking sheet and bake for 10 minutes.

6. Soften the chocolate ice cream for 15 minutes and spread it in the prepared pan into an even cake layer. Freeze for 30 minutes.

CHOCOLATE GANACHE FILLING

1. To prepare the ganache filling, place the chocolate chips and corn syrup in a heatproof bowl. In a small saucepan, heat the whipping cream just until it begins to boil, and then pour it over the semi-sweet chocolate chips and corn syrup. Let it sit for 2 minutes, and then stir with a spatula until the chocolate melts and becomes glossy.

2. Pour the prepared chocolate ganache over the chilled chocolate ice cream layer. Freeze for another 15 minutes.

3. Top with the prepared Oreo crumbs. Freeze the cake for at least 2 hours.

4. Soften the vanilla ice cream for 15 minutes and spread it on top of the frozen cake. Freeze for at least another 2 hours

ASSEMBLY

1. Once ready to serve, lift the cake from the pan using the plastic wrap.

2. You can decorate with swirls of buttercream and confetti sprinkles.

3. This cake should be frozen until it is ready to be served. It remains fresh in the freezer for about 3 days.

COFFEE & BUNDT CAKES

Baked just right!

MARBLE POUND CAKE   64

ORANGE CAKE WITH MASCARPONE   66

MOM-IN-LAW'S UPSIDE-DOWN PINEAPPLE CAKE   68

CHOCOLATE SHEET CAKE   70

STRAWBERRIES & CREAM SHEET CAKE   72

LOTUS (BISCOFF) BANANA BREAD   74

STICKY TOFFEE BUNDT CAKE   76

GINGERBREAD BUNDT CAKE   78

RED VELVET BUNDT CAKE   80

RAINBOW BUNDT CAKE   82

TUMERIC CAKE   84

KUNAFA CHEESECAKE   86

MARBLE POUND CAKE

Makes one 9-inch pound cake

Marble cake is one of my preferred ways to create a stunning layered cake that looks good on the inside as well as the outside. I once made a marble layered cake and took it over to my brother's house for a family gathering. My sister-in-law loved the design and suggested I make it as a one-layered pound cake, so I thought it would be fun to share in this book.

MARBLE POUND CAKE

2 cups (250g) flour

¼ tsp. salt

2 tsp. baking powder

1 cup (213g) unsalted butter, softened

⅛ cup (15g) cocoa powder

1⅓ cup (270g) sugar

2 tsp. vanilla extract

1 tsp. orange zest (optional)

3 eggs

½ cup (120ml) milk

MARBLE POUND CAKE

1. Preheat the oven to 350°F (180°C).

2. Spray a 9x5 pound cake pan and line it with parchment paper.

3. In a medium bowl, mix the flour, salt, and baking powder and set aside.

4. Melt 3 tablespoons of the butter in the microwave. Mix with the cocoa powder.

5. In the bowl of a stand mixer fitted with the paddle attachment, beat the remaining butter and sugar for a few minutes until light and fluffy.

6. Add the vanilla and orange zest and beat until combined.

7. Add the eggs one at a time and beat for another 2-3 minutes.

8. Start by adding a third of the flour mixture. Then add a third of the milk. Keep alternating between the flour and milk until both have been fully combined.

9. Split the cake batter into two bowls. Add the cocoa butter mixture into one of the bowls and mix very well until combined.

10. Start by putting the cocoa batter in the bottom of the pan. Top with the vanilla batter all over. Smooth out the vanilla batter using a spatula.

11. Cover with aluminum foil and bake for 30 minutes. Remove the aluminum foil and bake for another 25-30 minutes until a toothpick inserted in the center comes out almost clean.

12. Let the cake cool for 20 minutes before flipping over onto a wire rack to cool completely.

13. This cake can be stored at room temperature for up to 4 days.

ORANGE CAKE WITH MASCARPONE

Makes one 9-inch round cake

What I love about this cake is it comes out looking so rustic and chic. Hence, it's perfect for an afternoon tea rendezvous with friends or a family gathering. It is one-layered, so it is very easy to make and does not need any fancy decoration. If you are new to baking cakes, this would be a great place to start.

ORANGE CAKE

2 cups (250g) flour

1 tsp. baking powder

½ tsp. baking soda

¼ tsp. salt

2 tsp. fresh orange zest

¾ cup (180ml) canola oil

1 cup (200g) sugar

4 eggs

¾ cup (180ml) fresh orange juice

MASCARPONE FROSTING

1 batch mascarpone frosting, see
    recipe on page 163

ORANGE CAKE

1. Preheat the oven to 350°F (180°C).

2. Spray a 9-inch cake pan with baking spray and line with a parchment round.

3. In a medium bowl, mix the flour, baking powder, baking soda, salt, and orange zest.

4. In the bowl of a stand mixer fitted with the paddle attachment, beat the sugar and oil about 3 minutes until pale in color.

5. Add the eggs one at a time, mixing well after each addition. Beat for 2 minutes.

6. Start by adding a third of the flour mixture and alternate with a third of the orange juice. Keep alternating until all of the flour and juice are added. Beat just until combined.

7. Pour into the prepared cake pan.

8. Bake for 35-40 minutes until a toothpick inserted comes out clean.

9. Let the cake cool completely before flipping over a wire rack.

MASCARPONE FROSTING

1.   Make the mascarpone frosting. See page 163.

ASSEMBLY

1. Spread the mascarpone frosting on top of the cake and smooth it out using a spatula to create a rustic look.

2. You can leave the cake as is or decorate with candied oranges or slices of oranges and berries.

MOM-IN-LAW'S UPSIDE-DOWN PINEAPPLE CAKE

Makes one-layer 9-inch round cake

This is my mom-in-law's recipe. I tried this cake once when we were visiting Lebanon on vacation, and I fell in love with its light and fluffy texture. I couldn't take an Instagram-worthy picture at the time because it was baked as a wide one-layer cake, so I transformed this recipe into a three-layered cake as soon as I got the chance to try it at home.

PINEAPPLE CAKE

2 cups (250g) flour

1 ½ tsp. baking powder

1 Tbsp. (14g) unsalted butter

1 cup (200g) sugar (for the
pineapples)

1 can (20-oz.) (570g) pineapple slices

6 eggs, at room temperature

syrup from pineapple can

2 cups (400g) sugar (for the cake
batter)

1 tsp. vanilla extract

zest of one lemon

PINEAPPLE CAKE

1. Preheat the oven to 360°F (180°C).

2. Spray one 9-inch cake pan with baking spray.

3. Mix the flour and baking powder and set aside.

4. In a medium saucepan, place the butter over medium heat.

5. Add the cup of sugar and stir with a wooden spoon until it caramelizes into a golden color.

6. Pour the caramelized sugar into the prepared pan and top with the pineapple slices.

7. Using a stand mixer fitted with the whisk attachment, whisk the eggs for 4-5 minutes until frothy.

8. Add the pineapple syrup followed by the sugar, one cup at a time mixing well after each addition.

9. Add the vanilla and mix.

10. Add the flour mixture and mix just until combined.

11. Pour the cake batter into the prepared pan. Tap the pan on the kitchen counter to pop some of the air bubbles.

12. Bake for 30 minutes or until a toothpick inserted in the center comes out clean.

13. Let the cake cool completely in the pan before flipping over to a wire rack.

14. This cake can be stored at room temperature for 2-3 days.

CHOCOLATE SHEET CAKE

Makes one 9-inch sheet cake

I cannot resist how delicious a chocolate sheet cake smothered with luscious, glossy chocolate frosting looks. It is just too good, and, as a bonus, it is easy to make and much easier to decorate than a layered cake. This recipe results in a very moist and delicious sheet cake: perfect for starting on your baking journey.

CHOCOLATE SHEET CAKE

2 cups (250g) flour

⅔ cup (65g) cocoa powder

1 tsp. salt

1 tsp. baking soda

1 cup (240ml) buttermilk, at room
 temperature

½ cup Greek or natural yogurt

1 cup (227g) unsalted butter, melted

2 cups (400g) sugar

1 tsp. espresso powder

1 Tbsp. vanilla extract

2 Tbsp. (30ml) oil

3 eggs, at room temperature

CHOCOLATE FROSTING

1 batch chocolate frosting, see recipe
 on page 156

CHOCOLATE SHEET CAKE

1. Preheat the oven to 350°F (180°C).

2. Grease the bottom and sides of a 9x13 baking pan and line the bottom with parchment paper.

3. In a medium bowl, sift the dry ingredients (flour, cocoa powder, salt, and baking soda). Stir the mixture.

4. In another bowl, mix the buttermilk and Greek yogurt.

5. In the bowl of a stand mixer fitted with the paddle attachment, beat the butter and sugar for 3 minutes until light and fluffy. Add the espresso powder, vanilla, and oil and mix.

6. Add the eggs one at a time mixing well after each addition.

7. Reduce the mixer speed to low and start alternating between the flour and milk mixtures until all have been added in.

8. Pour the batter into the prepared pan and smooth the top with an offset spatula.

9. Bake for 35-40 minutes or until a toothpick inserted in the center comes out almost clean.

10. Let it cool completely in the pan before flipping over and frosting with the chocolate frosting.

CHOCOLATE FROSTING

1. Make a batch of chocolate frosting. See page 156.

STRAWBERRIES & CREAM SHEET CAKE

Makes one 9-inch sheet cake

This is the only recipe in the book that uses a cake mix as the base. While I am a fan of making cakes from scratch, I am a firm believer of trying everything out and of each baker finding the techniques that best suit their preferences. I really liked how this cake turned out with the cake mix, so I decided to stick to a box mix for this recipe rather than attempt to make it from scratch. I topped it with a vanilla strawberry Swiss meringue buttercream and fresh berries, and it reminded me of the many times I used to eat strawberries and cream as a kid!

STRAWBERRY SHEET CAKE

1 box Duncan Hines Strawberry
    Supreme cake mix (or any
    strawberry cake mix)

1 cup (240ml) buttermilk

3 eggs

½ cup (118ml) canola oil

1 tsp. vanilla extract

SWISS MERINGUE
BUTTERCREAM

1 batch Swiss meringue buttercream
    See recipe on page 155

pink gel food coloring

TOPPING

1 cup fresh strawberries, sliced

STRAWBERRY SHEET CAKE

1. Preheat the oven to 350°F (180°C).

2. Grease the bottom and sides of a 9x13 baking pan and line the bottom with parchment paper.

3. In the bowl of a stand mixer fitted with the paddle attachment, add the cake mix, buttermilk, eggs, canola oil, and vanilla extract and beat for a few minutes until well combined.

4. Pour the cake batter into the prepared pan. Bake in the preheated oven for 25-28 minutes or until a toothpick inserted in the center of the cake comes out clean.

5. Cool in the pan for 15 minutes then invert onto a wire rack to cool completely. Cover in plastic wrap and store at room temperature until ready to frost.

SWISS MERINGUE BUTTERCREAM

6. Make a batch of the vanilla Swiss meringue buttercream. See page 155. Add few drops of pink gel food coloring.

ASSEMBLY

1. Use an offset spatula to frost the top of the strawberry sheet cake with the buttercream. Create waves using the spatula.

2. Top with the fresh strawberries.

3. The frosted cake can be served immediately or stored in the fridge for 2 days.

LOTUS (BISCOFF) BANANA BREAD

Makes one 9-inch loaf

Banana Bread is one of the recipes that I, along with almost everyone I know, baked a lot during quarantine days. Every time, I did a small tweak to the classic recipe such as adding chocolate chips or spreads on top. For this recipe, I added scoops of Lotus spread on top of the Banana Bread batter in the loaf pan and swirled it around. It was the best decision I had ever taken. The result was a warm delicious Banana Bread where every bite kept you longing for more.

BANANA BREAD

2 cups (250g) flour

2 tsp. baking powder

½ tsp. baking soda

½ tsp. cinnamon

pinch of salt

2 eggs

1 tsp. vanilla extract

¼ cup (50g) sugar

½ cup (118ml) oil

3 ripe bananas, mashed

½ cup semi-sweet chocolate chips

4-5 small scoops Lotus (Biscoff) spread

BANANA BREAD

1. Preheat the oven to 350°F (180°C).

2. Spray a cake loaf pan with baking spray and line with parchment paper that goes up to the sides of the cake.

3. In a medium bowl, mix the flour, baking powder, baking soda, cinnamon, and salt. Set aside.

4. In the bowl of a stand mixer fitted with the whisk attachment, whisk the eggs, vanilla, and sugar at high speed for 2 minutes.

5. Add the oil and mix until combined.

6. Add the mashed bananas and mix.

7. Add the flour mixture and mix.

8. Add the chocolate chips and fold in using a spatula.

9. Pour the batter into the prepared cake pan.

10. Top with a bit more chocolate chips if desired.

11. Using an ice cream scoop, place 4 to 5 scoops of Lotus spread on top of the batter inches apart. Use a toothpick or large wooden stick and swirl the Lotus spread around the batter to create a beautiful shape.

12. Bake for 35 minutes or until a toothpick inserted in the center comes out clean. Let the loaf cool for 20 minutes before inverting onto a wire rack to cool completely.

STICKY TOFFEE BUNDT CAKE

Makes one 12-cup Bundt cake

Whenever I go back to visit my home country, I always have a reunion with my childhood best friends, Lama and Ghina, and we always go for a sushi dinner. After a delightful sushi meal and lots of catching up, we order two desserts for sharing, and one the desserts we order is a sticky toffee pudding. It is always so delicious and moist, so I had to recreate it at home, but in the form of a Bundt cake so the whole family can share.

BUNDT CAKE

2 cups pitted (375g) dates

2½ cups (600ml) water

2¾ cups (345g) flour

½ tsp. salt

2 tsp. baking powder

2 tsp. baking soda

½ cup (113g) unsalted butter, softened

1⅓ cups (267g) sugar

4 eggs

1½ tsp. vanilla extract

TOFFEE SAUCE

¾ cup (170g) unsalted butter

1 cup (200g) sugar

¾ cup (178ml) whipping cream

pinch of salt

1 tsp. vanilla extract

BUNDT CAKE

1. Preheat the oven at 350°F (180°C).

2. Grease the Bundt pan generously with baking spray. Sprinkle flour all over the sides of the pan and tap off the excess over the kitchen sink.

3. In a medium saucepan, place the dates and water over medium heat. Stir until it boils; then remove from the heat.

4. Use a potato masher to smash the date mixture until all the dates have melted and the mixture has a thick soup consistency. Set aside.

5. In a medium-sized bowl, add the flour, salt, baking powder, and baking soda. Set aside.

6. In the bowl of a stand mixer fitted with the paddle attachment, beat the butter for about 30 seconds until light and fluffy. Add the sugar and beat for a few minutes until the mixture is creamy.

7. Add the eggs one at a time, mixing well after each addition.

8. Scrape down the sides and mix for 30 seconds. Then add the the vanilla and mix.

9. Add the dates mixture and mix until combined.

10. Add the flour mixture and mix at low speed just until combined. Scrape down the sides and give the batter a final mix.

11. Pour the cake batter into the prepared Bundt pan.

12. Bake for 45-50 minutes or until a toothpick inserted in the center comes out clean.

13. Let the cake cool completely before inverting onto a wire rack.

TOFFEE SAUCE

1. In a saucepan over medium heat, mix the butter and sugar until the butter melts. Then leave the mixture without stirring and let it boil until it turns into a golden caramel color. This will take about 5 minutes.

2. Slowly and carefully add the whipping cream. Keeping your face and hands away, stir for 3-5 minutes until the sauce thickens (or until the temperature reaches around 212-216°F).

3. Remove off the heat. Add the salt and vanilla and stir just until combined.

4. Use immediately to drip all over the Bundt cake.

5. This cake can be stored at room temperature.

GINGERBREAD BUNDT CAKE

Makes one 12-cup Bundt cake

This is a cake I make every Christmas season. Incredibly moist, spiced to perfection, sweet, and delicious is all I can say about this cake. My husband can eat it all in one go even though he isn't really into spiced food.

GINGERBREAD BUNDT CAKE

2½ cups (345g) cake flour

2 cups (400g) sugar

2 tsp. ginger powder

1 tsp. cinnamon

1 tsp. salt

2 tsp. baking soda

1 tsp. baking powder

1 cup (240ml) buttermilk*, at room
    temperature

½ cup (120g) sour cream

½ cup (125ml) canola oil

⅓ cup (107g) molasses

½ cup (120ml) hot water

1 tsp. vanilla extract

1 tsp. white vinegar

2 eggs

GINGERBREAD BUNDT CAKE

1. Preeat the oven to 350°F (180°C).

2. Spray a Bundt cake pan generously with baking spray. Dust it off with flour and tap off the excess flour in the kitchen sink.

3. In the bowl of a stand mixer fitted with the paddle attachment, mix the flour, sugar, ginger powder, cinnamon, salt, baking soda, and baking powder.

4. In another medium bowl, mix the buttermilk, sour cream, oil, molasses, hot water, vanilla, and vinegar. Add the eggs, one at a time, mixing well after each addition.

5. Add the wet ingredients to the dry ingredients in the mixer bowl. Mix until well combined.

6. Bake for 50 minutes until a toothpick inserted in the center comes out clean. Start checking at 30 minutes.

7. Let cool in the pan for 20-30 minutes before flipping over on a wire rack to cool completely.

TIPS & TRICKS

* To make buttermilk at home, add 1 tablespoon fresh lemon juice to one measuring cup.
Fill the remainder of the cup with full fat milk. Leave it for 10 minutes. This produces one cup of buttermilk.

RED VELVET BUNDT CAKE

Makes one 12-cup Bundt cake

This cake was the first Bundt cake that I ever made. Prior to making it, I often read about common failures where the Bundt cake broke apart when it was being removed from the pan. I was determined not to let that happen, so I started off by spraying my Bundt pan generously with baking spray and dusting it with a lot of flour. I even recorded the moment of flipping the cake over and did a little happy dance when it came out in full. It was around Christmas time, and the video of my red velvet Bundt cake being flipped over with a Christmas song in the background went viral.

RED VELVET BUNDT CAKE

2½ cups (313g) flour

1½ cups (300g) sugar

1 tsp. baking soda

½ tsp. salt

2 Tbsp. cocoa powder

1 cup (240ml) buttermilk*

1½ cups (375ml) canola oil

2 eggs

1 tsp. white vinegar

2 tsp. vanilla extract

red food coloring

RED VELVET BUNDT CAKE

1. Preheat the oven to 350°F (180°C).

2. Grease the Bundt cake pan generously with baking spray. Sprinkle some flour all over the sides and bottom and tap off the excess over the kitchen sink.

3. In the bowl of a stand mixer fitted with the paddle attachment, mix the flour, sugar, baking soda, salt, and cocoa powder and set aside.

4. In another bowl, mix the buttermilk, oil, eggs, vinegar, vanilla, and red food coloring. The mixture should be bright red.

5. Add the wet ingredients (milk mixture) to the dry ingredients (flour mixture) and mix on low speed until slightly combined. Increase the speed to medium and mix for about 30 seconds until well combined. Scrape down the sides and mix for another 10 seconds.

6. Pour the cake batter to fill up ¾ of the prepared Bundt pan.

7. Bake 55-65 minutes. Start checking at 50 minutes until a toothpick inserted in the center of the Bundt cake comes out clean.

8. Remove the cake and let it cool for at least 20 minutes before flipping it slowly onto a cooling rack.

TIPS & TRICKS

* To make buttermilk at home, add 1 tablespoon fresh lemon juice to one measuring cup. Fill the remainder of the cup with full fat milk. Leave it for 10 minutes. This produces one cup of buttermilk.

RAINBOW BUNDT CAKE

Makes one 12-cup Bundt cake

This cake is so much fun to make, and all the pretty bright colors will add the most beautiful touch to any dessert (or dinner!) table. Don't want a rainbow cake? No problem! Skip the colors (step 8) and make it a delicious vanilla Bundt cake.

RAINBOW BUNDT CAKE

3 cups (375g) flour

6 Tbsp. cornstarch

2 tsp. baking powder

1 tsp. salt

1½ cups (339g) unsalted butter, softened

2 cups (400g) sugar

4 eggs

1 Tbsp. vanilla

½ tsp. almond extract

1 cup (240ml) full fat milk

gel food colors (red, orange, yellow, green, blue, purple)

RAINBOW BUNDT CAKE

1. Preheat the oven to 350°F (180°C).

2. Grease the Bundt pan generously with baking spray. Sprinkle flour all over and tap off the excess.

3. In a medium bowl, whisk the flour, cornstarch, baking powder, and salt. Set aside.

4. In the bowl of a stand mixer fitted with the paddle attachment, beat the butter and sugar until light and fluffy.

5. Add the eggs one at a time beating well after each addition.

6. Add the vanilla and almond extracts and mix.

7. Add half of the flour mixture and mix. Add half the milk and mix until combined.

8. Continue alternating between the remaining flour and milk mixtures and mix just until combined. Scrape down the sides and give it a final mix.

9. Split the cake batter into 6 small bowls. Add 2 drops of each of the gel colors to each bowl and fold just until combined.

10. Pour the colorful cake batter (one color after the other) into the prepared Bundt pan and smooth the top with a spatula.

11. Bake for 55 minutes or until a toothpick inserted in the middle comes out clean.

12. Let cool in the pan for 15-20 minutes before inverting onto a cooling rack to cool completely.

TURMERIC CAKE

Makes one 8-inch square cake

Although this was a classic dessert I had regularly growing up, the first time I ever tried making this cake was when I was asked to create a Levantine dessert for a TV show. The first thing that came to mind was the famous sfouf, aka turmeric cake. This cake recipe is simple and straightforward, and it can be whipped up in less than 30 minutes if the right ingredients are available. My version is a bit on the lighter side compared to the ones sold at sweet shops.

TURMERIC CAKE

1½ cups coarse semolina

½ cup (62g) flour

1 Tbsp. turmeric powder

1½ tsp. baking powder

½ cup (108ml) canola oil

1 cup (240ml) full fat milk

1 cup (200g) sugar

TOPPING

pine nuts or almond halves for
    decoration

TURMERIC CAKE

1. Preheat the oven to 350°F (180°C).

2. Generously spray a 9-inch square pan with baking spray and line with parchment paper.

3. Mix the semolina, flour, turmeric powder, and baking powder. Set aside.

4. In a separate bowl, mix the canola oil, milk, and sugar.

5. Add the wet ingredients to the dry ingredients and mix just until combined.

6. Pour the cake batter into the prepared pan and sprinkle the pine nuts on top.

7. Bake 30-35 minutes. Start checking at 20 minutes. If a toothpick inserted in the center comes out with only a few crumbs, the cake is ready. Decorate with pine nuts or almond halves.

KUNAFA CHEESECAKE

Makes one single-layer 9-inch cake

Kunafa is a very popular dessert in the Middle East and loved all around the world. It is mainly made with a vermicelli dough, stuffed with either cheese or fresh cream, and baked until golden perfection. I wanted to make a twist on the classic recipe, so I decided to turn it into a no-bake cheesecake. The combination of the baked Kunafa crust soaked with syrup and the creamy frozen cheesecake is just divine.

SUGAR SYRUP

1 cup (200g) sugar

½ cup water

1 tsp. orange blossom

1 tsp. rose water

KUNAFA CHEESECAKE CRUST

4 cups Kunafa dough

⅓ cup (67g) sugar

½ cup (113g) unsalted butter

KUNAFA CHEESECAKE FILLING

2 cups (454g) cream cheese, softened

2 cups (480ml) whipping cream

⅓ cup (67g) sugar

2 tsp. rose water

2 tsp. orange blossom

1 tsp. vanilla extract

SUGAR SYRUP

1. In a medium saucepan, place the sugar, water, orange blossom, and rose water over medium heat. Stir until the sugar dissolves and then leave the mixture to boil.

2. Once it boils, leave it for 10 minutes exactly. Then remove it immediately off the heat.

3. Pour it into bowl and set aside to cool.

KUNAFA CHEESECAKE CRUST

1. Preheat the oven to 350°F (180°C).

2. Place a parchment round into a 9-inch springform pan.

3. In a large bowl, break up the Kunafa dough into smaller pieces.

4. Add the sugar and butter and rub them together until the butter coats the Kunafa dough well.

5. Press the Kunafa dough into the bottom of the prepared pan using a cup until it forms a firm even layer.

6. Bake the crust in the pre-heated oven for 20-30 minutes until golden. Let it cool for a few minutes only and then pour the sugar syrup all over the crust while it is still hot.

KUNAFA CHEESECAKE FILLING

1. In the bowl of a stand mixer fitted with the paddle attachment or using an electric mixer, beat the cream cheese for 1-2 minutes until creamy.

2. Add the vanilla extract, rose water, and orange blossom and beat for 30 seconds.

3. Add the whipping cream and beat for about 2 minutes at medium speed.

4. Finally, add the sugar and mix for another minute.

ASSEMBLY

1. Spread the cheesecake filling over the baked Kunafa crust. Smooth with an offset spatula.

2. Freeze for at least two hours. The longer it is frozen, the better the cheesecake will hold its shape when served.

3. This cake can be decorated with more Kunafa dough. Just add some butter and stir it over medium heat until it is golden. Let it cool and sprinkle it over the cheesecake.

COOKIES & BARS

Cookies make the world a better place!

CHOCOLATE SUGAR COOKIES 90

JAM SABLÉ COOKIES 92

PEANUT BUTTER COOKIES 94

CHOCOLATE-DIPPED VIENNESE COOKIES 96

BROWNIE COOKIES 98

BROWNIES 100

COOKIE CAKES 102

CHOCOLATE SUGAR COOKIES

Makes 22 medium-sized cookies

I have a weakness for chocolate bakes, chocolate cake, chocolate donuts, and, of course, chocolate sugar cookies. They remind me of the chocolate petit fours that my mom used to make for us at home all the time when we were young. I once topped these cookies with chocolate frosting, and I have never looked back. They look and taste incredible, so I had to include the recipe in the book because it's too good not to share.

CHOCOLATE SUGAR COOKIES

3¾ cups (470g) flour

¾ cup (85g) unsweetened cocoa
    powder

½ tsp. salt

1½ cups (335g) unsalted butter,
    softened

1½ cups (300g) sugar

1 egg, cold

2 tsp. vanilla extract

CHOCOLATE FROSTING

1 batch of chocolate frosting
    (optional), see recipe on page 156

CHOCOLATE SUGAR COOKIES

1. In a medium bowl, mix the flour, cocoa powder, and salt together. Set aside.

2. In the bowl of a stand mixer fitted with the paddle attachment, beat the butter and sugar for about 1 minute until light and fluffy.

3. Scrape down the sides of the bowl and add the egg. Mix just until combined.

4. Add the flour mixture gradually until it is incorporated.

5. Add the vanilla extract and mix to form a dough.

6. Divide the dough into two equal parts. Place a nonslip mat on the kitchen counter and sandwich the dough between two pieces of parchment paper.

7. Using a rolling pin, roll the disk into a large rectangle and place on the back of a baking sheet. Place back in the fridge and chill for 1 hour or overnight.

8. Remove the chilled cookie dough and cut out cookies using cookie cutters.

9. Preheat the oven to 325°F.

10. Line three baking sheets with parchment paper.

11. Freeze the cut-out shapes for another 15 minutes.

12. Place the cookies into the oven and bake for about 15 minutes just until the borders are set. Cookies will continue to bake in the hot baking sheet.

13. Let the cookies cool slightly in the baking sheet and place on a wire rack to cool completely.

CHOCOLATE FROSTING

1. Make a batch of chocolate frosting. See page 156.

JAM SABLÉ COOKIES

Makes 10 cookies

This is another childhood treat that was often available at home while I was growing up. In Lebanon, these cookies were usually sold in an assortment cookie box containing different sorts of petit fours. While everyone else always went first for the chocolate petit fours (which I also loved), I was one who went for the vanilla cookies with apricot jam. This cookie recipe is my attempt at recreating some of these beautiful memories.

COOKIES

1 cup (226g) unsalted butter, softened

3 cups (375g) flour

1¼ cups powdered sugar

¼ tsp. vanilla extract

2 egg yolks

½ cup apricot jam

COOKIES

1. In the bowl of a stand mixer fitted with the paddle attachment, beat the butter, flour, powdered sugar, vanilla, and egg yolks until the mixture forms a cohesive dough that sticks to one side of the bowl.

2. Cover the dough with plastic wrap and chill in the fridge for one hour.

3. In the meantime, line 2 baking sheets with parchment paper.

4. Once chilled, place the dough between two sheets of parchment paper and roll using a rolling pin. You can place the parchment paper on a nonslip mat while rolling to prevent the dough from slipping.

5. Chill the dough for another 15 minutes.

6. Pre-heat the oven at 350°F (180°C).

7. Press a round cookie cutter in flour and cut the cookies. Place the cut cookies immediately over the prepared baking sheets. Use a round piping tip to cut a circle in the center of half of the cut cookies.

8. Bake the cookies for 15-18 minutes, only until slightly golden around the edges.

9. Let the cookies cool for 15 minutes. Then place them on a wire rack to cool completely.

ASSEMBLY

1. Scoop a ½ teaspoon of apricot jam on top of each full cookie circle.

2. Top with the cut cookie. Sprinkle the cookies with powdered sugar.

*NOTE: These cookies stay fresh in an airtight container for a few days

PEANUT BUTTER COOKIES

Makes 14 medium-sized cookies

Peanut butter is one of my favorite ingredients especially for breakfast and for adding into my desserts. That is why you will always find me experimenting new dessert recipes using Peanut Butter. These cookies are one of those examples and I love how soft these cookies turned out.

PEANUT BUTTER COOKIES

1⅓ cups (170g) flour

1 tsp. baking powder

1 tsp. salt

⅔ cup (85g) unsalted butter, melted

½ cup + 1 Tbsp. (113g) brown sugar

½ cup (100g) sugar

1 egg, cold

1 cup (250g) creamy peanut butter

1 tsp. vanilla extract

PEANUT BUTTER COOKIES

1. Preheat the oven to 350°F (180°C).

2. Line 2 baking sheets with parchment paper.

3. In a medium bowl, whisk the flour, baking powder, and salt. Set aside.

4. In the bowl of a stand mixer fitted with the paddle attachment, beat the butter and both sugars until light and fluffy.

5. Add the egg and mix.

6. Add the peanut butter and vanilla and mix.

7. Add flour mixture and mix just until combined.

8. Use an ice cream scooper to scoop out balls of dough. Place them on the baking sheets inches apart.

9. Use a fork to make cross diagonal lines at the top of the cookie balls. Clean the fork between each cookie to get clean ridges.

10. Bake for 10 minutes just until the edges are golden. For soft and chewy cookies, do not overbake.

11. Place a round cookie cutter almost the same size of the cookie on top of each cookie (while still warm) and swirl the cookie inside to create perfect circle shapes.

12. Let the cookies cool in the sheets for 10-15 minutes before transferring them onto a wire rack to cool completely.

13. These cookies can be stored in an airtight container at room temperature for a few days.

CHOCOLATE-DIPPED VIENNESE COOKIES

Makes 14 cookies

These cookies are one of the cookies I grew up eating back home. My grandma always had a box of this type of cookies with different flavors and fillings. Such as jam and chocolate This homemade version tastes much better than the commercial ones in my grandma's cookie box and I make them so my children can create similar beautiful memories with food while growing up.

VIENNESE COOKIES

1 cup (230g) unsalted butter, softened

6 Tbsp. (47g) powdered sugar

2 tsp. vanilla extract

2⅓ cups (300g) flour

½ cup (100g) semi-sweet chocolate
   chips (for dipping)

VIENNESE COOKIES

1. Preheat the oven to 350°F (180°C).

2. Line two baking sheets with parchment paper.

3. In the bowl of a stand mixer fitted with the paddle attachment, beat the butter and sugar until the mixture is soft.

4. Add the vanilla and mix.

5. Add the flour gradually and beat until combined and smooth. The texture will be thick, so keep beating until it becomes smoother and pipeable.

6. Pour the batter into a piping bag fitted with a star piping tip (example: Wilton 1M).

7. Pipe the desired cookie shapes. To pipe rosettes, start piping in the center and move anti-clockwise starting and ending at the 3 o'clock position.

8. Bake for 12 minutes just until slightly golden around the edges.

9. Let cool in the pan for a few minutes and then transfer onto a wire rack to cool completely.

ASSEMBLY

1. Melt the chocolate chips in the microwave in 30 second intervals. Let cool slightly.

2. Once the cookies and the melted chocolate have cooled, dip one end of the cookies in the melted chocolate. Place back on the wire rack until the chocolate sets.

3. Cookies can be stored in an airtight container for a few days.

BROWNIE COOKIES

Makes 10 large cookies

As you will read in the next recipe, Brownies is one of my top desserts so a brownie cookie version was a must try recipe and the result was a crinkly chocolate cookie that resembled a brownie in cookie form. They are so fun to make and equally as fun to eat with a cold cup of milk.

BROWNIE COOKIES

1 cup (125g) flour

1 tsp. baking powder

pinch of salt

⅓ cup (85g) unsalted butter, softened

1 cup (190g) semi-sweet chocolate
   chips

¼ cup (24g) unsweetened cocoa
   powder

1 tsp. espresso powder

2 eggs

1 egg yolk

1 cup (200g) sugar

1 tsp. vanilla extract

1 Tbsp. canola oil

BROWNIE COOKIES

1. Preheat the oven to 350°F (180°C).

2. Line two baking sheets with parchment paper.

3. In a medium bowl, whisk the flour, baking powder, and salt. Set aside.

4. In a saucepan over medium heat, heat the butter and chocolate chips until melted. Remove from heat and sift in the cocoa and espresso powders. Whisk until combined. The mixture will be thick.

5. In the bowl of a stand mixer fitted with the paddle attachment, beat the eggs, egg yolks, sugar, vanilla extract, and oil together until combined.

6. Add the melted chocolate mixture and mix just until combined.

7. Add the flour mixture and mix just until combined.

8. Use an ice cream scooper and scoop the cookie dough into the prepared sheets.

9. Bake for 8-9 minutes.

10. Let cool in the baking sheet for a few minutes. Then transfer to a wire rack to cool completely.

11. Cookies can be stored in an airtight container for 5 days.

BROWNIES

Makes 9 brownie slices

Brownies are one of my favorite desserts. I'll always order a brownie if I am having desserts outside of home (which happens often). I love having brownies with a hot cup of cappuccino. This recipe creates coffee-shop-style brownies with a cracked crust. I also like to fancy it up with some biscuits, but that is totally optional.

BROWNIES

1 cup (185g) semi-sweet chocolate
   chips, melted

1 cup (100g) flour

¼ cup (24g) unsweetened cocoa
   powder

½ tsp. salt

½ cup + 2 Tbsp. (140g) unsalted
   butter, melted

1 cup (200g) sugar

2 eggs, at room temperature

2 tsp. vanilla extract

9 round biscuits (such as Oreos)
   (optional)

BROWNIES

1. Preheat the oven to 350°F (180°C).

2. Line a 9x5 baking sheet with baking spray and parchment paper.

3. Place the chocolate chips in a heatproof bowl and heat in the microwave for 30 second intervals (30 seconds, stir, another 30 seconds, stir—repeat until melted). Set aside to cool.

4. In a medium bowl, sift the flour, cocoa powder, and salt and set aside.

5. Melt the butter for 30 seconds in the microwave.

6. Add the sugar to the melted butter and, using a hand whisk, whisk until well combined.

7. Add the eggs one at a time, mixing well after each addition.

8. Add the vanilla and mix again.

9. Add the melted chocolate and mix until combined.

10. Add the flour mixture and whisk just until well combined.

11. Pour the batter into the prepared pan.

12. If using biscuits, place 9 biscuits evenly across the brownie pan and press them into the batter so that, when cut later, each square slice gets one biscuit.

13. Bake the brownies for around 30 minutes. Start checking at around 25 minutes. When a toothpick comes out almost clean, the brownies are ready. If you prefer more gooey brownies, you can take them out before that.

14. Let the brownies cool for at least 30 minutes in the pan. Then use the parchment paper to lift out the pan onto a wire rack. Let cool completely.

15. Use a sharp bread knife to cut the brownies into 9 even squares.

COOKIE CAKES

Makes 6 two-tiered medium cookie cakes

These mini cookie cakes are perfect for events like baby showers and birthdays. You can apply this technique to any cookie shapes you want as long as you can stack them up. You can decorate them either with fresh or edible flowers, sprinkles, or fresh berries. The cookie world is as wide as your imagination!

COOKIES

4¾ cups (565g) flour

½ tsp. salt

1½ cups (339g) unsalted butter, softened

1½ cups (300g) sugar

1 egg, cold

1 tsp. vanilla extract

SWISS MERINGUE BUTTERCREAM

1 batch of Swiss Meringue Buttercream, see recipe on page 155

TOOLS

1 large and 1 small round cookie cutter (2cm difference in size)

COOKIES

1. In a medium bowl, mix the flour and salt and set aside.

2. In the bowl of a stand mixer fitted with the paddle attachment, cream the butter and sugar until creamy for just 2 minutes.

3. Scrape down the sides of the bowl. Add the egg and mix just until combined.

4. Add the vanilla extract and mix until combined. Add the flour mixture and beat just until it forms a recognizable dough.

5. Divide the dough into 2 equal parts. Shape each part into a disc by pushing it down with the palm of your hand.

6. Place a nonslip mat on the kitchen counter. Top with a large parchment paper. Top with the first dough disc. Top with another parchment paper.

7. Roll the cookie dough using a rolling pin ensuring the dough is of an even thickness throughout. Repeat with the second dough disc.

8. Chill the rolled dough in the fridge for 30 minutes or overnight.

9. When ready to bake, preheat the oven to 325 °F.

10. Use a large round cookie cutter to cut large cookie circles. Then using a small round cookie cutter, cut a hole in the center to create a donut shaped cookie.

11. Lift the cookies gently and place them on the prepared baking sheet inches apart as cookies will slightly expand during baking. Place them in the freezer to chill for 15 minutes.

12. You can re-roll the leftover cookie dough one more time and chill it to create more cookies.

13. Bake in the preheated oven for 10-12 minutes just until slightly golden around the edges. Cookies will continue to bake in the hot baking sheet.

14. Let the cookies cool for 15 minutes before moving them onto a wire rack to cool completely.

SWISS MERINGUE BUTTERCREAM

1. Make a batch of Swiss Meringue Buttercream. See page 155.

ASSEMBLY

1. Fill a piping bag fitted with a round piping tip (such as Wilton 1A) with the vanilla Swiss meringue buttercream.

2. Place one of the round cookie shapes on a mini cake board or a plate. Pipe small round kisses of the buttercream on top and go around to cover the entire cookie. Cover very gently with another cookie. Pipe the top of the cookie with another round of buttercream dollops.

3. Chill for 10-15 minutes so the buttercream firms up a bit.

4. You can decorate these cookies with sprinkles, edible dust, edible flowers, fresh florals, and gold leaf. As these cookies are covered with buttercream, they need to be stored in the fridge until ready to serve.

MACARONS

A ready-to-eat piece of heaven!

MACARONS

When it comes to macarons, I have so much to share with you, to teach you. Like so many others, I felt intimidated by making macarons for a long time and first attempted them in December 2019, six years after beginning my baking journey. Yes, that is how long it took me to get the courage to try them, but that does not have to be the case for you. With my foolproof recipe and the tips, tricks, and things to avoid that I will share with you in this book (that I usually share in my online macarons classes), you will be set for a success probability of 95% the first time and a probability of 100% by your next attempt. These tips have proven successful for many of students who have taken my online macarons classes, and that is why I am so confident they will work for you too.

I will first talk all about preparation, tips, and tricks before sharing my basic recipe and a couple of flavor recipes. I encourage you to follow all the tips shared to the letter to ensure your success in making these finicky cookies.

PREPARATION

- One of the first tips is to separate your egg whites from the egg yolks (per the quantity called for in the basic French macarons recipe) while the eggs are still cold. This needs to be done 4 hours before you plan to begin making the macarons. It is extremely important that the macarons are at room temperature.

- Prepare your baking sheets and line them with the silicone baking mats. I highly advise investing in macarons silicone baking mats. I have seen much better results using them than using parchment paper.

- Sift and measure the dry ingredients (almond flour and powdered sugar) and set them aside until ready to start making the macarons.

- Use a 16-inch piping bag fitted with a coupler first. Then add a round piping tip on the outside (example: Wilton tip 12). Set aside until the macarons batter is ready.

- You will need the following tools:

  1. Kitchen scale
  2. Oven thermometer (optional but may help)
  3. Sieve to sift the dry ingredients
  4. 16-Inch piping bag
  5. Coupler and round piping tip
  6. Silicone baking mat or parchment paper
  7. Scissors
  8. 2-3 Baking sheets
  9. Stand or electric mixer and bowl (whisk attachment)
  10. Rubber spatula

TIPS & TRICKS

There are two main tips which I believe make my recipe a success from the very first time:

- Baking at a low temperature: My recipe calls for baking the macarons at 285°F. This helps prevent most of the issues that bakers face when making macarons (example: cracked shells or concave-shaped macarons). Baking at a low temperature helps the macarons to rise slowly, helping create those beautiful signature feet of macarons.

- "Under-mixing" the batter: As humans, we always tend to stir or mix a little more than necessary. When we put it in our mindset to under-mix, we will mix it just enough instead of over-mixing. If you overmix the batter at this stage, the batter will be very runny, and the macarons will not get nice feet. They will bake flat. Hence, what I have found useful since day 1 of baking macarons is under-mixing the batter just until it is right; You will stop mixing when you reach what we call the ribbon stage, as you will read in the recipe.

Here are some other tips that also help in getting perfect macaron shells:

- Tap the macarons sheet over the kitchen counter a couple of times after piping. This will remove the air bubbles trapped in the macarons batter. If you skip this step, you will get hollow (empty) shells.
- Use silicone baking mats instead of parchment paper (as I have mentioned previously).
- Use an oven thermometer to test your oven temperature and make sure it is only at 285°F at the time of baking.
- Preheat the oven only after you have piped the macarons.
- Do not skip the step of resting the macarons after piping. This will create a skin on the shells that will prevent them from cracking during baking in the hot oven.
- Let the macarons cool completely before peeling the mat away from the macarons.
- After filling the macarons, keep them in the fridge overnight. This helps them become even more full.
- Macarons stay fresh for a few days in the fridge and up to 3 months in the freezer (shells only for freezing).

FRENCH MACARONS

Makes around 22 macaron shells

INGREDIENTS

145 grams egg whites , at room temperature

1⅓ cups (125g) almond flour, sifted

2⅛ cups (240g) powdered sugar, sifted

1/3 cup (75g) sugar

1 tsp. vanilla extract

few drops gel food coloring (optional)

white vinegar for wiping the tools

DIRECTIONS

1. Prepare a large baking sheet and line it with a macarons silicone mat or parchment paper.

2. Separate the egg whites while the eggs are still cold. Let the egg whites sit at room temperature on the kitchen counter for 3-4 hours.

3. Sift the almond flour as you measure it into a bowl using a fine sieve. Then, sift the powdered sugar as you measure it on top of the almond flour. Mix them gently with a spoon and set aside.

4. Wipe the bowl of the mixer and the whisk attachment with white vinegar. This will make sure there are no butter or oil residues to prevent the egg whites from whipping up.

5. In the bowl of a stand mixer fitted with the whisk attachment, add the egg whites. Start beating at low speed for two minutes.

6. Once little bubbles appear at the top, add the white sugar gradually. Add the vanilla extract. Mix for two minutes at low speed. Turn the speed to medium and whisk for another two minutes.

7. Turn the mixer speed to high and beat for a few minutes until it becomes thicker and whiter in color (shaving cream consistency) Add a little gel food coloring at this point.

8. Turn the mixer speed back to high and beat until you get stiff peaks. The mixture becomes white and glossy. If you lift the whisk off, the mixture does not fall off the whisk and has a pointed peak. If the peak is still inclined, it means it is not yet ready. Beat it for a few more minutes until you get a very pointy peak. Do not beat beyond this point.

9. Add the egg white mixture to the almond/powdered sugar mixture prepared earlier and, using a spatula, start folding the mixture in. Fold the mixture from the bottom upwards and push it gently to the sides. Stop folding as soon as a ribbon forms when you lift off the spatula or if you try to write the number 8 with the spatula, it disappears within 3 seconds. Do not overbeat or your batter will be runny and the macarons will not get nice feet.

10. Prepare a piping bag with a coupler and round tip. Using a tall cup, place the piping bag and pour the macaron batter in. Then cut the bag open with scissors.

11. Place your hand with the piping bag 90 degrees above the prepared sheet and start piping your macarons starting in the center and letting the circle form following the mat template. End each circle as if you are writing a comma before moving to pipe the next circle.

12. After piping, tap the baking sheet over your kitchen counter a couple of times. Air bubbles will appear at the top of some of the shells. Wiggle these air bubbles gently with a toothpick to get a smooth finish.

13. Preheat the oven to 285°F (140°C).

14. Rest the piped macarons for 25-30 minutes or until no batter sticks to the finger when touched. Another sign for readiness is the macarons becoming matte-like and losing their shine. It may take more than 30 minutes depending on the weather and kitchen temperature.

15. Bake the macarons one tray at a time for 18-20 minutes. They should have risen and have nice feet.

16. The macarons are ready when they lift off the mat smoothly without sticking. You could try peeling the mat from the bottom away from one of the macaron shells to test them. If it does not lift off and is still sticking to the mat, it means you need to bake the macarons for a few more minutes. Place the sheet back in the oven and bake them slightly longer. Let the macarons cool completely before peeling them away from the sheet.

CHOCOLATE MACARONS

Makes around 22 macaron shells

Macarons are one of the things that when I bake, I have to try on the spot. They are simply irresistible. Make it chocolate macarons, and you would see me sitting at the stove top and snacking on one shell after the other. Once you have mastered the classic French macarons recipe, I suggest you give this a try. I am sure you are going to love it.

INGREDIENTS

145g egg whites , at room temperature

1¼ cups (114g) almond flour, sifted

2 cups (230g) powdered sugar, sifted

⅛ cup (16g) unsweetened cocoa powder

⅜ cup (75g) sugar

1 tsp. vanilla extract

white vinegar for mixing tools

DIRECTIONS

1. Prepare a large baking sheet and line it with a macarons silicone mat or parchment paper.

2. Separate the egg whites while the eggs are still cold. Let the egg whites sit at room temperature on the kitchen counter for 3-4 hours.

3. Sift the almond flour as you measure it into a bowl using a fine sieve. Then, sift the powdered sugar as you measure it on top of the almond flour. Finally, sift the cocoa powder on top. Mix them gently with a spoon and set aside.

4. Wipe the bowl of the mixer and the whisk attachment with white vinegar. This will make sure there are no butter or oil residues to prevent the egg whites from whipping up.

5. In the bowl of a stand mixer fitted with the whisk attachment, add the egg whites. Start beating at low speed for two minutes.

6. Once little bubbles appear at the top, add the white sugar gradually. Add the vanilla extract. Mix for two minutes at low speed. Turn the speed to medium and whisk for another two minutes.

7. Turn the mixer speed to high and beat for a few minutes until it becomes thicker and whiter in color (shaving cream consistency).

8. Turn the mixer speed back to high and beat until you get stiff peaks. The mixture becomes white and glossy. If you lift the whisk off, the mixture does not fall off the whisk and has a pointed peak. If the peak is still inclined, it means it is not yet ready. Beat it for a few more minutes until you get a very pointy peak. Do not beat beyond this point.

9. Add the egg white mixture to the almond/powdered sugar/ cocoa powder mixture prepared earlier and, using a spatula, start folding the mixture in. Fold the mixture from the bottom upwards and push it gently to the sides. Stop folding as soon as a ribbon forms when you lift off the spatula or if you try to write the number 8 with the spatula, it disappears within 3 seconds. Do not overbeat or your batter will be runny and the macarons will not get nice feet.

10. Prepare a piping bag with a coupler and round tip. Using a tall cup, place the piping bag and pour the macaron batter in. Then cut the bag open with scissors.

11. Place your hand with the piping bag 90 degrees above the prepared sheet and start piping your macarons starting in the center and letting the circle form following the mat template. End each circle as if you are writing a comma before moving to pipe the next circle.

12. After piping, tap the baking sheet over your kitchen counter a couple of times. Air bubbles will appear at the top of some of the shells. Wiggle these air bubbles gently with a toothpick to get a smooth finish.

13. Preheat the oven to 285°F (140°C).

14. Rest the piped macarons for 25-30 minutes or until no batter sticks to the finger when touched. Another sign for readiness is the macarons becoming matte-like and losing their shine. It may take more than 30 minutes depending on the weather and kitchen temperature.

15. Bake the macarons one tray at a time for 18-20 minutes. They should have risen and have nice feet.

16. The macarons are ready when they lift off the mat smoothly without sticking. You could try peeling the mat from the bottom away from one of the Macaron shells to test them. If it does not lift off and is still sticking to the mat, it means you need to bake the macarons for a few more minutes. Place the sheet back in the oven and bake them slightly longer. Let the macarons cool completely before peeling them away from the sheet.

S'MORES MACARONS

Makes around 11 S'mores Macarons

Do you love s'mores everything? Yay! We can be best friends. I love s'mores ice cream, cakes, cupcakes and especially the recipe I am sharing here, macarons! Here is a recipe that will impress anyone with your baking skills. Once you have mastered my basic macarons recipes, you are ready to take over the macaron world!

MACARONS

1 batch of chocolate macaron shells
   see recipe on page 112

MARSHMALLOW FILLING

white vinegar

150g egg whites

2 cups (400g) sugar

¼ cup (60ml) water

¼ tsp. cream of tartar

1 tsp. vanilla extract

TOPPING

1 batch of chocolate ganache, dipping
   consistency, see recipe on page 157

MACARONS

1. Make a batch of the chocolate macaron shells. See page 112.

MARSHMALLOW FILLING

1. Wipe the bowl of a stand mixer, whisk attachment, and a spatula with white vinegar. Then, add the egg whites, sugar, water, and cream of tartar.

2. Place the mixer bowl over a saucepan with simmering water. The bottom of the mixer bowl should not touch the water.

3. Stir the mixture using a spatula until it reaches 140°F on a candy thermometer.

4. Remove from the heat and place the whisk attachment.

5. Whisk the mixture at medium high speed until it becomes white and glossy and holds medium to stiff peaks. It should be stable enough to be piped.

6. Scoop the marshmallow filling into a piping bag fitted with a round tip (such as Wilton 1A).

7. Pipe small dollops of the marshmallow filling on top of a chocolate macarons shell and cover with another macarons shell. Repeat with the remaining shells. Place the filled macarons in the fridge to chill for about 1 hour.

CHOCOLATE GANACHE

1. Make a batch of the chocolate ganache and let it set only for 5 minutes. See page 157.

ASSEMBLY

1. Line a baking sheet with parchment paper.

2. Dip half of each chilled macaron into the chocolate ganache and lay on the baking sheet for the ganache to set.

3. Chill the macarons in airtight container until you are ready to serve them.

4. Filled macarons should be stored in the fridge and consumed within 3-4 days.

FANCY BERRY MACARONS

Makes around 10 large berry macarons

This recipe uses my basic French Macarons made in larger size and then filled with a swirl of buttercream and fresh berries. I use raspberries but you can replace these with sliced strawberries or even cherries. They make an excellent mini dessert idea. My husband , Sami, once told me these would be perfect if served as indidivual desserts at a fancy restaurant and hence the name "Fancy Berry Macarons".

FANCY BERRY MACARONS

1 batch of French macaron shells, see recipe on page 110

SWISS MERINGUE BUTTERCREAM

½ batch of Swiss meringue buttercream, see recipe on page 155

pink gel food coloring

TOPPING

1 cup fresh raspberries

gold leaf (optional)

1. Make a batch of the French macaron shells. See page 110.

1. Make 1/2 a batch of Swiss meringue buttercream. See page 155.
2. Color the buttercream with a few drops of the pink gel food color. Mix using a mixer or a spatula.

1. Scoop the buttercream into a piping bag fitted with a round tip (such as Wilton 1A).
2. Place one large macaron shell on a mini gold cake board if available.
3. Pipe two round circles of the pink buttercream in the middle.
4. Place berries upwards all around the piped buttercream.
5. Top and close with another macaron shell.
6. Repeat with the remaining macaron shells.
7. Top with gold leaf, if using.

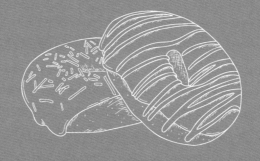

SWEET TREATS

You are what you eat, so eat something sweet!

ÉCLAIRS 120

MINI TARTS 122

TIRAMISU 124

PROFITEROLES 126

CHOCOLATE BALLS 128

CHURROS 130

ÉCLAIRS

Makes 12-14 mini éclairs

Here is another recipe that was a favorite for my whole family growing up. Whenever we had special guests coming over, my mom would buy half a dozen or dozen of these to be served with coffee and tea. I never imagined that once I grew up, I would be able to make these delicious French pastries at home. I have done a lot of research and this recipe along with the tips provided will result in beautiful éclair shells even before filling and dipping.

ÉCLAIRS

½ cup (100g) unsalted butter

½ cup (125ml) water

½ cup (125ml) full fat milk

1 tsp. sugar

pinch of salt

1¼ cups (150g) flour

4 eggs

PASTRY CREAM

1 batch of pastry cream, see recipe on
    page 162

CHOCOLATE GANACHE

1 batch of chocolate ganache, see
    recipe on page 157

TOOLS

piping bag

perforated baking mat (optional)

French star tip (example: Wilton 4B
    or 6B)

Wilton piping tip 230 for filling (or
    any small round tip)

ÉCLAIRS

1. Line 2 baking sheets with parchment paper.

2. Preheat the oven to 425°F.

3. In a medium saucepan over medium heat, add the butter, water, milk, sugar, and salt. Stir it with a wooden spoon until the butter melts. As soon as it starts to boil, reduce the heat and add the flour.

4. Stir vigorously until it forms a coherent dough. The bottom and sides of the pan will be clean when you pull it out.

5. Transfer the dough to a stand mixer fitted with the paddle attachment and let it cool for 15 minutes.

6. Add the eggs one at a time while beating at low speed until the mixture is smooth and when lifted off, it drops smoothly.

7. Transfer the choux dough into a piping bag fitted with a French star tip.

8. Pipe the éclairs' shapes on the prepared baking sheets inches apart. Sprinkle with powdered sugar.

9. Bake the éclairs for 25-30 minutes. Then reduce the heat to 375°F (190°C). Rotate the pan and bake for another 15 minutes. The éclairs are done when they are golden in color (not too brown).

10. Let the baked éclairs cool on the baking sheet for about 10 minutes.

11. In the meantime, prepare the pastry cream and the chocolate ganache.

PASTRY CREAM

1. Make a batch of pastry cream. See page 162.

2. Transfer the pastry cream into a piping bag fitted with the round tip (example: Wilton 230 or 12). Poke holes in each of the edges of the bottom of each éclair. Pipe the pastry cream in each hole until the piping tip is pushed out. Do not overfill them.

CHOCOLATE GANACHE

1. Make a batch of chocolate ganache. See page 157.

ASSEMBLY

1. Dip each éclair's top in chocolate ganache. Place over a wire rack for the chocolate to set.

2. Éclairs are best eaten on the same day they are filled. You can make the éclair choux dough a day or two before and fill them on the day of your event. They can be stored in an airtight container in the fridge.

MINI TARTS

Makes 5 mini tarts

Mini tarts are a great addition to dessert tables at birthdays and events. I love making them when I am organizing an outdoor event in my garden such as a baby shower or one of my kids' birthday parties. My favorite filling to eat with mini tarts is Chocolate Ganache but these shells can be filled with anything your heart desires such as Pastry Cream, Lemon Curd, and/or fresh fruits. Once you make the shells, you are in for a lot of fun.

MINI TARTS

1½ cups (185g) flour

½ cup (65g) powdered sugar

pinch of salt

½ cup (113g) unsalted butter, cubed
    and cold

1 egg

½ tsp. vanilla extract

raw chickpeas or rice as pie weights

CHOCOLATE GANACHE

1 batch of chocolate ganache, see
    recipe on page 157

TOPPINGS

fresh raspberries

powdered sugar

TOOLS

pastry cutter (optional)

perforated silicone mat

4 tart rings/molds

pizza cutter

piping bag

round piping tip (Wilton 1A)

MINI TARTS

1. In a medium bowl, mix the flour, powdered sugar, and salt. Set aside.

2. Mix the butter into the flour using hands or a pastry cutter until it resembles coarse sand.

3. Add the egg and continue mixing.

4. Add the vanilla extract and mix.

5. Once the dough becomes coherent, form it into a disc and cover with plastic wrap. Chill in the fridge for 1 hour.

6. Line a baking sheet with the perforated baking mat. Spray the tart rings with baking spray.

7. Sprinkle flour on the kitchen counter and roll the tart dough until it is about ¼ inch thick.

8. Use the tart ring to cut the tart round. Cut a long strip of dough using a pizza cutter and use it to cover the sides of the dough. Use your fingers to smooth out the dough into one tart base. Using a fork, prick the bottom of the tarts and place in the freezer for 25 minutes.

9. Preheat the oven to 350°F (180°C).

10. Place a parchment paper on the tart rings and top with the raw chickpeas.

11. Bake for 20 minutes. Remove the parchment paper and chickpeas and place in the oven again for 5 minutes. The tart should be golden.

12. Let cool completely before lifting the tart ring and filling with the pastry cream or ganache.

CHOCOLATE GANACHE

1. Make a batch of chocolate ganache. See page 157.

ASSEMBLY

1. After making the chocolate ganache, let it set for 5 minutes and then pour the into the prepared tart shells.

2. Top with fresh berries and dust with powdered sugar.

3. You can also fill the tart shells with pastry cream.

TIRAMISU

Makes one 4-inch tiramisu tray

This is my go-to, easy, no-bake tiramisu for those days I am craving one of my favorite desserts but not in the mood to spend long hours in the kitchen (which is a rare occasion but can happen). All you need is a batch of my homemade custard, and you are all set. The result is a creamy and light tiramisu that tastes great with your morning coffee or afternoon tea.

TIRAMISU

250g mascarpone cheese

2 Tbsp. vanilla extract

¾ cup (200ml) coffee, cold

20 lady fingers

1 Tbsp. cocoa powder

HOMEMADE CUSTARD

½ batch (250g) of homemade custard,
   see recipe on page 161

HOMEMADE CUSTARD

1. Make 1/2 a batch of homemade custard. See page 161.

TIRAMISU

1. Using an electric mixer, beat the mascarpone, custard, vanilla extract, and one tablespoon of the coffee for 3 minutes until light and fluffy.

ASSEMBLY

1. Dip the lady fingers one at a time in the coffee and place them in a tray.

2. Spoon half of the creamy mixture on top of the lady fingers and dust half of the cocoa powder.

3. Repeat with another layer of dipped lady fingers, creamy mixture and a final dust of cocoa powder.

4. Chill until ready to serve.

5. TIP: Do not dip the lady fingers in the coffee for too long so they do not get too soggy.

PROFITEROLES

Makes 24 small profiteroles

Here is another dessert I grew up eating at many family events in Lebanon, such as cousins' birthdays, weddings, and the like. We definitely like our desserts back home; they represent a major part of our celebrations, so it is no surprise that I grew up with a passion to create delicious desserts. I like to pile profiteroles into a "mountain" form, which would make the perfect addition to any dessert table at a family event. Regardless of your baking skill level, you can make choux that will still look pretty and taste incredibly delicious.

PROFITEROLES

½ cup (100g) unsalted butter

½ cup (125ml) water

½ cup (125ml) full fat milk

1 tsp. sugar

pinch of salt

1¼ cups (50g) flour

4 eggs

1 batch pastry cream

1 batch chocolate ganache

TOOLS

piping bag

round piping tips (Wilton 1A)

star piping tip (Wilton 1M)

INSTRUCTIONS

1. Preheat the oven to 350°F (180°C). Line 2 baking sheets with parchment paper.

2. In a medium saucepan over medium heat, add the butter, water, milk, sugar, and salt. Stir it with a wooden spoon until the butter melts. As soon as it starts to boil, reduce the heat and add the flour.

3. Stir vigorously until it forms a coherent dough. The bottom and sides of the pan will be clean when you pull it out.

4. Transfer the dough to a stand mixer fitted with the paddle attachment and let it cool for 15 minutes.

5. Add the eggs one at a time while beating at low speed until the mixture is smooth and when lifted off, it drops smoothly. Transfer into a piping bag fitted with a round piping tip.

6. Pipe blobs of the choux dough inches apart. Place some clean water on your finger and tap the pointy peaks of the piped choux.

7. Bake the choux for 20-25 minutes until they are golden all over.

8. In the meantime, prepare the pastry cream. You can even prepare the pastry cream a day before. Place the pastry cream in a piping bag fitted with a round piping tip.

9. Prepare the chocolate ganache for dipping the profiteroles' tops. Once baked, let the profiteroles cool in the pan.

ASSEMBLY

1. Poke a hole at the bottom of each profiterole using a round piping tip. Pipe the pastry cream into each hole until the tip pulls out.

2. Dip the top of the dipped profiteroles in chocolate ganache and let them set.

   *NOTE: Once filled, profiteroles are best served on the same day they are prepared.

CHOCOLATE BALLS

Makes 10 medium chocolate balls

While researching ideas for recipes to include in this book with my best friend, she insisted that I include another childhood favorite of ours: the chocolate ball. This was a staple in every pastry shop around our city back home. It is so easy to make and tastes so decadent. If you are looking for a quick sweet fix, this is a great choice.

CHOCOLATE BALLS

1¼ cups (200g) semi-sweet chocolate chips

25 (250g) chocolate biscuits , crushed (without the filling)

½ cup (37g) coconut powder

1 can (10.4-oz.) (397g) sweetened condensed milk

1 cup chocolate sprinkles

CHOCOLATE BALLS

1. Melt the chocolate chips in the microwave in 30 second intervals. Set aside to cool.

2. Line a baking sheet with parchment paper.

3. In a medium bowl, combine the crushed biscuits and coconut powder.

4. Add the condensed milk and melted chocolate and stir.

ASSEMBLY

1. Use a large ice cream scooper to create the balls and then, using wet hands, roll each ball to get a perfect round shape. Roll each ball in a bowl of chocolate sprinkles and place on the prepared baking sheet.

2. Chill in the fridge for 20 minutes before serving.

3. These may be stored in an airtight container in the fridge for a few days.

CHURROS

Makes 12-15 churros

Mexican cuisine is one of my favorite cuisines, but my real love for churros began during one of my trips to Disneyland. Churros are one of the most popular treats sold at Disneyland, and I fell in love with them from the first bite.

CHURROS

½ cup (40g) unsalted butter

⅔ cup (150ml) water

1½ Tbsp. (20g) sugar

¼ tsp. cinnamon

1 cup (110g) flour

2 eggs

3 cups canola oil for frying

TOPPING

½ cup (100g) sugar

½ tsp. cinnamon

½ batch chocolate ganache

TOOLS

kitchen thermometer

piping bag

star tip (Wilton 1M)

CHURROS

1. In a medium saucepan over medium heat, combine the butter, water, sugar, and cinnamon. Let the mixture melt and come to a boil. Then reduce the heat to low.

2. Add the flour and stir the dough using a spatula vigorously until it forms a cohesive dough ball. Once well combined, remove the dough off the heat. Transfer it to a stand mixer and let it cool before adding the eggs.

3. Once cooled, add the eggs one by one, mixing well at low speed after each addition.

4. Once the dough is smooth and combined, you are ready to start frying. Spoon the dough into a piping bag fitted with the star tip.

5. Place the canola oil in the saucepan and heat until it reaches 350°F (180°C).. While the oil is heating, pipe about 3cm-long (or any length you like) strips of the dough into parchment paper. Cut around the churros and place them in the oil with the parchment paper.

6. Fry the churros until they are golden brown on all sides. Once the churros start frying, the parchment paper will pull away and you can take them out with tongs or a ladle.

7. Transfer the golden churros onto paper towels to absorb the oil.

TOPPING

1. Mix the sugar and cinnamon for the topping. Dip the warm churros in the mixture and coat all sides generously.

2. Serve with chocolate ganache or any dipping of choice.

3. Churros are best eaten on the same day.

HOLIDAY BAKING

Christmas cookie calories don't count!

CHRISTMAS SUGAR COOKIES 135

GINGERBREAD COOKIES 138

HOT COCOA COOKIES 140

GINGERBREAD CAKE 142

BÛCHE DE NOËL (YULE LOG) CAKE 145

CHOCOLATE STARS TART 148

REINDEER & SNOWMEN MACARONS 150

CHRISTMAS SUGAR COOKIES

Makes 20 medium-sized cookies

Along with a basic chocolate cake, sugar cookies are one of the first things that I learned to bake. I read a lot of techniques and tips and watched so many videos to learn what could possibly go wrong and how best to avoid it. Here, I share with you all these tips so you can make perfect sugar cookies that maintain shape during baking.

CHRISTMAS SUGAR COOKIES

6 cups (750g) flour

1 tsp. salt

2 cups (454g) unsalted butter, softened

2 cups (400g) sugar

2 eggs, cold

2 tsp. vanilla extract

DECORATE WITH FONDANT

Fondant

DECORATE WITH BUTTERCREAM

Make a batch of buttercream, see recipes on pages 154 and 155

CHRISTMAS SUGAR COOKIES

1. In a large bowl, sift the flour and salt using a fine sieve and set aside.

2. In the bowl of a stand mixer fitted with the paddle attachment, beat the butter and sugar for around 2 minutes until light and fluffy. Do not overbeat; this will help the cookies maintain shape during baking.

3. Scrape down the sides of the bowl and add the eggs one at a time. Mix until combined.

4. Add the flour mixture gradually, mixing on low speed.

5. Add the vanilla extract and mix well until it forms a coherent cookie dough.

6. Divide the dough with your hands into two equal parts. Shape each part into a round disk and press it with your palms.

7. Place a nonslip mat on the kitchen counter followed by a large piece of rectangular parchment paper.

8. Place one of the cookie dough discs on top. Then cover it with another large rectangular parchment paper. Use a rolling pin and roll the cookie dough into an even thickness. The cookies should not be too thick or too thin.

9. Place the rolled cookie dough on the back of a cookie sheet or chopping board and slide into the fridge. Chill the rolled cookie dough for at least 35 minutes or overnight.

10. Pull out one cookie dough sheet from the fridge and cut out cookies using your chosen cookie cutters.

11. Preheat the oven to 350°F (180°C)..

12. Freeze the cut-out shapes for another 15 minutes.

13. Bake the cookies for 10-12 minutes just until the outside edges of the cookies are golden. Remember that cookies will continue to cook in the pan, so always remove them a minute or two before your preferred cookie color.

14. Let the cookies cool in the pan for about 15 minutes and then transfer them onto a wire rack to cool completely.

15. Decorate with fondant or any of the buttercream recipes in this book.

TO DECORATE WITH FONDANT

1. Knead the fondant by hand for a few minutes to make it pliable.

2. Sprinkle corn flour or powdered sugar over a silicone mat and roll the fondant using a fondant rolling pin until it is about ½ inch thick.

3. Cut the same shape of the cookie being decorated.

4. Use a kitchen brush to paint the back of the cut fondant shape with a very small amount of water (or edible glue if available). Carefully place the cut fondant on the cookie.

5. If the edges of the cookie are showing slightly, you can extend the fondant using a fondant smoother.

TO DECORATE WITH BUTTERCREAM

1. Make a batch of any buttercream recipe provided in this book.

2. Transfer the buttercream into a piping bag fitted with your chosen piping tip. My favorite tips for decorating cookies are Wilton 1M, 2B, 4B and 6B. You can also use small star tips, such as 18 and 21. More tips will be provided in the last chapter of the book, "Creating Showstopping Cakes."

3. Chill the decorated cookies and take out of the fridge 20-30 minutes before serving, depending on the temperature of your kitchen.

TIPS & TRICKS

* The dough chilling steps are essential for ensuring the cookies maintain their shape while baking.

* Unfrosted cookies can be stored in an airtight container for up to 10 days.

GINGERBREAD COOKIES

Makes 10 gingerbread cookies

Gingerbread cookies are also one of the first bakes that I learned how to make back when I started baking in 2013. I love creating Christmas-themed desserts, and I start doing that in early November every year. Gingerbread cookies are a great and easy way to create Christmas-themed desserts, but feel free to make them all year round. Just cut your favorite cookie shapes and enjoy!

GINGERBREAD COOKIES

3¼ cups (407g) flour

½ tsp. salt

1½ tsp. cinnamon

1½ tsp. ginger

⅓ tsp. allspice

½ tsp. baking soda

⅔ cup (142g) unsalted butter, softened

½ cup + 1 Tbsp. (110g) brown sugar

1 egg, cold

½ cup (110ml) molasses

1 tsp. vanilla extract

GINGERBREAD COOKIES

1. In a medium bowl, sift the flour, salt, spices, and baking soda. Set aside.

2. In the bowl of a stand mixer fitted with the paddle attachment, cream the butter and brown sugar for about 3 minutes until light and fluffy.

3. Add the egg, beating just until combined.

4. Add the molasses and mix. Add the vanilla extract and mix until combined.

5. Add the flour mixture and beat at low speed until it forms a coherent dough.

6. Divide the cookie dough into two parts. Shape each part into a disc and press with the palm of your hands. Cover with plastic wrap and chill for 1 hour.

7. Place a piece of nonslip mat on the kitchen counter followed by a large piece of rectangular parchment paper. Sprinkle some flour.

8. Place one of the dough discs on top. Then, cover it with another large rectangular parchment paper. Use a rolling pin and roll the dough into an even thickness.

9. Place the rolled cookie dough on the back of a cookie sheet or chopping board and slide into the fridge. Chill the rolled cookie dough for 35 minutes.

10. Preheat the oven to 350°F (180°C). Line 2 baking sheets with parchment paper.

11. Pull out the rolled dough from the fridge and cut out cookies using your chosen cookie cutters.

12. Freeze the cut-out shapes for another 15 minutes.

13. Bake the cookies for 8-12 minutes just until the edges of the cookie start to brown.

14. Let the cookies cool in the pan for 15 minutes and transfer onto a wire rack to cool completely.

15. These cookies can be eaten and served as is or decorated with royal icing and sprinkles. They can be stored in an airtight container for up to one week.

HOT COCOA COOKIES

Makes 12 medium cookies

For me, hot cocoa is a holiday staple, whether as the classic hot chocolate drink topped with lots of mini marshmallows, in the form of a fun cake, or, in this case, as cookies. These are my go-to chocolate cookies. They are filled generously with marshmallows, making them the perfect holiday treat for the entire family.

HOT COCOA COOKIES

10 regular-sized marshmallows

1 cup (125g) flour

½ cup (50g) cocoa powder

½ tsp. baking soda

¼ tsp. salt

¼ cup + 1 Tbsp. (57g) semi-sweet
    chocolate chips

½ cup (113g) unsalted butter, softened

⅔ cup (135g) brown sugar

⅓ cup (67g) sugar

1 egg, cold

1 tsp. vanilla extract

½ cup (85g) semi-sweet chocolate
    chips

HOT COCOA COOKIES

1. Slice each marshmallow in half at the center and place in the freezer.

2. In a medium bowl, whisk the flour, cocoa powder, baking soda, and salt. Set aside.

3. Melt the chocolate chips in the microwave in 30 second intervals and let them cool.

4. In the bowl of a stand mixer fitted with the paddle attachment, beat the butter and both sugars until light and fluffy for about a minute.

5. Add the cooled chocolate and beat for 30 seconds.

6. Add the egg and vanilla extract and beat just until combined.

7. Scrape down the sides of the bowl and add the flour mixture over two batches. Beat at low speed and add the second batch. Beat just until combined.

8. Add the chocolate chips and beat at low speed for 20 seconds.

9. Cover the cookie dough bowl in plastic wrap and chill in the fridge for at least 2 hours.

10. Preheat the oven to 350°F (180°C). Line 2 baking sheets with parchment paper.

11. Use a large ice cream scooper to scoop out a large ball of the chocolate cookie dough. Dampen your hands with water and make an indent in the center of the dough.

12. Place half of a frozen marshmallow in the center. Then roll the cookie into a ball and close it. Repeat with the remaining cookie dough.

13. Place the cookies 2 inches apart on the baking sheet and bake in the preheated oven for 10-12 minutes. Do not overbake so the cookies stay gooey.

14. Let the cookies cool in the pan for 10 minutes before transferring them onto a wire rack to cool completely.

15. These cookies can be stored in an airtight container for up to 5 days.

GINGERBREAD CAKE

Makes one three-layer 6-inch cake

The holiday season is all about gingerbread everything, so a gingerbread cake is a must on everyone's baking list. In this recipe, I transformed my gingerbread Bundt cake into a layered cake and paired it with cinnamon cream cheese frosting for an extra richness in flavor .

GINGERBREAD CAKE

2¾ cups (345g) cake flour*

2 cups (400g) sugar

2 tsp. ginger powder

1 tsp. cinnamon

1 tsp. salt

2 tsp. baking soda

1 tsp. baking powder

1 cup buttermilk**

½ cup (120g) sour cream

½ cup (125ml) canola oil

⅓ cup (107g) molasses

½ cup (120ml) hot water

1 tsp. vanilla extract

1 tsp. white vinegar

2 eggs

CINNAMON CREAM CHEESE FROSTING

½ cup (113g) unsalted butter, softened

1 cup (226g) cream cheese, softened

1 tsp. vanilla extract

¼ tsp. salt

¼ tsp. cinnamon

4 cups (500g) powdered sugar

GINGERBREAD CAKE

1. Preheat the oven to 350°F (180°C).

2. Spray three 6-inch cake pans with baking spray and line with parchment rounds.

3. In the bowl of a stand mixer fitted with the paddle attachment, mix the flour, sugar, ginger powder, cinnamon, salt, baking soda, and baking powder.

4. In another medium bowl, mix the buttermilk, sour cream, oil, molasses, hot water, vanilla, and vinegar. Add the eggs one at a time, mixing well after each addition.

5. Add the wet ingredients to the dry ingredients in the mixer bowl. Mix until well combined.

6. Divide the cake batter evenly among the prepared cake pans using a kitchen scale.

7. Bake for 30-35 minutes or until a toothpick inserted in the center comes out clean.

8. Let the cakes cool in the pan for 25 minutes before inverting onto a wire rack to cool completely.

9. Wrap in plastic wrap and keep in the fridge until ready to frost.

CINNAMON CREAM CHEESE FROSTING

1. In the bowl of a stand mixer fitted with the paddle attachment, beat the butter and cream cheese for 2-3 minutes until smooth.

2. Add the vanilla extract, salt, and cinnamon and beat for another 2 minutes.

3. Add the powdered sugar gradually and beat at high speed for 5 minutes until the frosting is smooth and creamy.

4. Reduce the speed to low and beat for 5 minutes to remove the air bubbles.

ASSEMBLY

1. Trim the cake tops. Fill the cake layers with the cinnamon cream cheese frosting. Cover the top and sides of the cake with a thin layer of the frosting. Smooth the sides using a cake scraper and chill for at least 30 minutes.

2. Cover with a final layer of frosting. You can decorate with gingerbread cookies in any shape using Christmas-themed cookie cutters.

TIPS & TRICKS

*To make cake flour at home, measure 2½ cups flour. Remove 5 tablespoons of the flour and replace them with 5 tablespoons of corn starch. Sift and measure 2¼ cups from this mixture.

* To make buttermilk at home, add 1 tablespoon fresh lemon juice to one measuring cup. Fill the remainder of the cup with full fat milk. Leave it for 10 minutes. This produces one cup of buttermilk.

BÛCHE DE NOËL (YULE LOG) CAKE

Makes one yule log cake

This is my mom's favorite cake ever. She even asks me to make it outside of the holiday season. I remember Dad buying it for us during the Christmas season or on New Year's Eve. It was such a fancy treat. Never did I imagine that I would successfully recreate it at home. Rolling a cake can be intimidating, but with the tips I am going to share with you, you will most likely get it right from the first try !

YULE LOG CAKE

2 Tbsp. (16g) flour

½ cup (50g) unsweetened cocoa powder

½ tsp. salt

5 eggs, whisked

⅔ (133g) cup sugar

½ tsp. vanilla extract

2 Tbsp. melted butter

CHOCOLATE GANACHE

1 batch of chocolate ganache, see recipe
    on page 157

CHOCOLATE FILLING

1½ cups (360ml) whipping cream

¼ cup (25g) unsweetened cocoa powder

¼ cup (50g) sugar

YULE LOG CAKE

1. Preheat the oven to 390°F (200°C).

2. Line a large baking sheet with parchment paper.

3. In a small bowl, sift the flour, cocoa powder and salt. Set aside.

4. In the bowl of a stand mixer fitted with the whisk attachment (or electric hand mixer), add the eggs, sugar, and vanilla extract. Whisk the mixture until it becomes lighter in color. When the whisk is lifted, the batter drops, creating a ribbon shape.

5. Add the flour mixture. Whisk slowly for about 10 seconds, then whisk on medium speed for another 10 seconds until the flour is well incorporated.

6. Brush a thin layer of melted butter all over the parchment paper. This will ensure the cake sponge does not stick during baking.

7. Pour the cake batter into the prepared baking sheet, leaving a little space at the edges. If the baking sheet is too small, you can divide the batter into two baking sheets.

8. Tap the baking sheet on the kitchen counter a couple of times to remove the air bubbles.

9. Reduce the oven temperature to 360°F (180°C). Bake for about 10 minutes or until a toothpick inserted in the center comes out clean.

10. Let the cake cool in the baking sheet for a few minutes. Then sprinkle powdered sugar using a small sieve all over the top. Flip the cake over a big tea towel.

11. Carefully and slowly peel off the parchment paper from the top of the cake. Then using the tea towel at the base, gently and slowly roll the cake sponge into a cake roll. Let it rest while still rolled inside the tea towel for 15 minutes.

12. After 15 minutes, unroll the cake and fill with a thin layer of the filling.

13. Roll the cake back. Cover in plastic wrap and chill for at least one hour until it firms up.

CHOCOLATE FILLING

1. Place a medium bowl in the freezer for 5 minutes.

2. Using an electric mixer, whisk the whipping cream in the chilled bowl for at least 5 minutes until it thickens and forms stiff peaks.

3. Add the cocoa powder and sugar and whisk until combined.

4. This chocolate Yule log stays fresh in the fridge for about 2 days.

CHOCOLATE GANACHE

1. Make a batch of the chocolate ganache and let it thicken slightly into a spreadable consistency. See page 157.

ASSEMBLY

1. Once the cake has chilled well, cut a small slice diagonally at the edge. That will be used as the branch of the "log". Stick the cut piece in the center of the cake roll using a little bit of the chocolate ganache.

2. Using a small offset spatula, cover the cake roll fully with the ganache. Let it set in the fridge for at least 15 minutes.

3. To decorate, take the cake roll out of the fridge and use a small knife to create a branch texture. Sprinkle a bit of powdered sugar using a small sieve to create snow-like effect. Chill until ready to serve.

CHOCOLATE STARS TART

Makes one 12-inch tart

Once you have mastered making the tarts recipe provided in this book, you can create beautiful tarts in various sizes. For the holidays, I like to create a big tart filled with chocolate ganache and decorated with gold sugar cookies. The gold against the chocolate color creates a beautiful effect that is perfect for the holidays or any time of the year.

CHOCOLATE TART

1½ cups (188g) flour

½ cup (62g) powdered sugar

¼ tsp. salt

½ cup (113g) unsalted butter, cubed and cold

1 egg

½ tsp. vanilla extract

raw chickpeas or rice as pie weights

CHOCOLATE GANACHE

1 batch of chocolate ganache, see recipe on page 157

TOPPINGS

few star-shaped sugar cookies, see page 103

white sugar paste (fondant)

gold lustre powder

lemon extract

2 fresh rosemary twigs (optional)

TOOLS

pastry cutter (optional)

large tart pan

pizza cutter

2 small food-safe brushes

CHOCOLATE TART

1. In a medium bowl, mix the flour, powdered sugar, and salt. Set aside.

2. Mix the butter into the flour using hands or a pastry cutter until it resembles coarse sand.

3. Add the egg and continue mixing.

4. Add the vanilla extract and mix.

5. Once the dough becomes coherent, form it into a disc and cover with plastic wrap. Chill in the fridge for 1 hour.

6. Spray the tart pan with baking spray.

7. Sprinkle flour on the kitchen counter and roll the tart dough until it is about ¼ inch thick.

8. Place the rolled tart dough on the rolling pin and transfer it into the prepared tart pan. Position the dough properly in the center of the pan. Trim off the excess on the edges of the tart using a small sharp knife. Using a fork, prick the bottom of the tarts and place in the freezer for 30 minutes. This will help the tart maintain shape during baking.

9. Preheat the oven to 350°F (180°C).

10. Place a parchment paper on the rolled tart dough and top with the raw chickpeas/pie weights.

11. Bake for 20 minutes. Remove the parchment paper and chickpeas and place in the oven again for 5 minutes. The tart should turn golden in color.

12. Let cool completely before lifting from the tart pan.

CHOCOLATE GANACHE

1. Prepare the chocolate ganache from page 157 and let it set for 5 minutes. Pour into the prepared and cooled tart shell. Let it set in the fridge for 15 minutes.

ASSEMBLY

1. Cut out star shapes out of white sugar paste using the same cutter that was used to make the star sugar cookies. Stick the cut stars on top of the cookies using a bit of water or edible glue. (You can make the cookies using the same recipe used for the mini cookie cakes on page 103).

2. Mix a pinch of the gold lustre powder with about 1/8 teaspoon lemon extract until it has a paint-like consistency. Use a medium brush to paint the star cookies and then let them dry at room temperature. The cookies can be prepared a day or two in advance.

3. Once the chocolate ganache has fully set, place the gold star cookies on top. You can also decorate with some fresh rosemary twigs.

REINDEER & SNOWMEN MACARONS

Makes 11 snowmen macarons and 11 reindeer macarons

You cannot let the holidays pass without creating cute snowmen or reindeer dessert treats. These macarons are not only cute but also make the perfect baking activity to do with the kids while on the long winter break.

SNOWMEN MACARONS

1 batch of white French macarons, baked
and filled (check steps for notes), see
recipe on page 110

SNOWMEN MACARONS FILLING

1 batch of Swiss meringue buttercream,
see recipe on page 155

SNOWMEN MACARONS TOPPINGS

orange sugar paste (fondant)

edible black pen

REINDEER MACARONS

1 batch of chocolate or brown French
macarons, baked and filled, see recipes
on page 112 or page 110

REINDEER MACARONS FILLING

1 batch of chocolate frosting, see recipe
on page 156

REINDEER MACARONS TOPPINGS

⅜ cup (60g) semi-sweet chocolate chips
(or good quality chocolate) or mini
pretzels

edible black pen

red/pink confetti sprinkles or red
buttercream

SNOWMEN MACARONS

1. To get white macarons, prepare the French macarons as indicated in the French macarons recipe on page 110 without adding any food color. Bake them for 10 minutes then slide the tray out and cover the top of the macarons with a rectangular strip of aluminum foil, making sure not to smash the macarons. This will help keep the color white and prevent the macarons from burning. Bake them for another 8-10 minutes until they are ready. Remove the aluminum foil carefully as soon as they are out of the oven.

2. You can use Swiss meringue buttercream on page 155 to fill the snowmen macarons. Swiss meringue buttercream is not overly sweet, so it balances out the sweetness of the macaron shell. Once the macarons are baked and filled, they are ready to decorate.

3. Roll a small piece of the orange sugar paste into a small nose shape for the snowman.

4. Stick it in the center of the white round macaron. You can also just use an orange edible marker for this step.

5. Draw two dots for the eyes with the edible black pen. The orange nose should be below and centered between the eyes.

6. At the bottom of the orange nose, draw a few black dots to create a smiling face for the snowman.

REINDEER MACARONS

1. Make a batch of chocolate macarons, see recipe on page 112. You can use chocolate frosting on page 156 to complement the chocolate shell flavor.

2. Melt the semi-sweet chocolate chips in the microwave in 30 second intervals. The chocolate should not be too runny. Place in a piping bag without any piping tip. Cut a very thin opening in the piping bag.

3. Draw two dots using the black edible pen for the reindeer eyes. You can also draw unicorn-style lashes instead of the eyes.

4. Stick a red or pink round confetti sprinkle as the reindeer nose using a bit of water or edible glue.

5. For the reindeer antlers, pipe very small antler (branch) shapes on top of each eye dot using the melted chocolate. Let the chocolate set. If this step is too complicated, you can just use mini pretzels cut in half and insert them in the inside while you are filling the macarons to create the antler shapes. Let the filled Macarons set in the fridge so the antlers do not move.

BUTTERCREAM, CAKE FILLINGS & FROSTINGS

The best things in life are sweet!

AMERICAN BUTTERCREAM

American buttercream is the first buttercream I ever experimented and started playing around with in the world of cake decorating. While my most preferred buttercream to decorate cakes is the Swiss meringue buttercream, this is a close second. I use this recipe regularly when creating content because it is so easy to make and the consistency is perfect for frosting smooth cakes with sharp edges.

INGREDIENTS

2 cups (450g) unsalted butter, softened

5 cups (560g) powdered sugar

1 tsp. vanilla extract

few drops gel food color (optional)

DIRECTIONS

1. In the bowl of a stand mixer fitted with the paddle attachment, beat the butter at high speed for about 5 minutes until light and fluffy.

2. Add the powdered sugar all at once and beat at low speed until well combined. Then beat at high speed for a minute.

3. Add the vanilla extract and beat for 30 seconds at low speed.

4. Add the gel color and beat for 2 minutes at medium speed.

5. Increase the speed to high and beat for at least 5 minutes. Then reduce the speed to the lowest speed and beat for 5 minutes. This will help reduce the air bubbles. To further reduce the air bubbles, use a rubber spatula and beat the buttercream by hand for a few minutes.

6. Scoop the buttercream into a piping bag and set aside until you are ready to decorate your cake.

STORAGE

1. American buttercream is best prepared on the day the cake will be eaten. However, it can be stored in the fridge for one week or in the freezer for about 2 weeks.

2. To store the buttercream, place it in a closed piping bag or airtight container.

3. Once you are ready to use the buttercream, place the container at the kitchen counter for about 30 minutes to 1 hour depending on the temperature of your kitchen. Then place the buttercream in the bowl of a stand mixer fitted with a paddle attachment and beat for 5 minutes until the consistency comes back to smooth and spreadable. Reduce the speed to low and beat for 5 minutes to remove the air bubbles.

SWISS MERINGUE BUTTERCREAM

This is my go-to buttercream in about 99% of the cakes I bake and decorate. It is so smooth and creamy and is perfect for getting smooth cakes. In addition, it is not overly sweet, and I have received positive feedback from many people stressing the importance of this and how they loved that my cakes were not as sweet as other cakes they were used to. This recipe is just enough to fill and cover a three-layer 6-inch cake. To add piping details to the cake, make an extra ½ batch on top of this. You can double the recipe by multiplying each ingredient by 2.

INGREDIENTS

200g egg whites (from 6 large eggs)

1½ cups (300g) sugar

1¾ cups (400g) unsalted butter, softened

½ tsp. vanilla extract

TIPS & TRICKS

*Swiss meringue buttercream can be kept at room temperature for 2-3 hours while the cake is being decorated. It can be stored in the fridge in an airtight container for one week or in the freezer for 3 weeks. To defrost, place the buttercream in the fridge the night before. Then take it out and place it at room temperature for one hour. Use a stand mixer with the paddle attachment to beat it and bring back the silky-smooth consistency.

DIRECTIONS

1. First, start by wiping the following tools with white vinegar using a kitchen or paper towel: stand mixer bowl, whisk attachment, spatula, medium saucepan, small bowl.

2. While the eggs are cold, separate the egg whites from the yolks. Separate each egg white in the small bowl first and transfer it to the saucepan. If a little egg yolk comes into the mixture, try to remove it carefully using a clean eggshell.

3. Add the sugar to the egg whites. Mix using the spatula.

4. Place the saucepan over medium heat. Keep stirring until the sugar dissolves and the mixture reaches 147°F (64°C) on a digital candy thermometer. If a digital candy thermometer is not available, you can check the readiness by touching a bit of the mixture and rubbing it between your fingers. If you no longer feel sugar particles, the mixture is ready and can be removed off the heat.

5. Transfer the mixture to the bowl of the stand mixer. Use a sieve when transferring to remove any potentially cooked egg whites.

6. Using the whisk attachment, beat the mixture on medium-high speed for 5-10 minutes. The mixture will double in volume and become white and glossy. You should immediately reduce the speed once the mixture reaches the "stiff peak" stage. If you lift off the whisk, there should be a pointy white peak that does not wiggle and is stable.

7. Once the speed is reduced to low, start adding the butter, about a tablespoon at a time, until all the butter has been added in. Mix for a few more minutes at medium-high speed.

8. Switch to the paddle attachment and continue beating at medium-high speed until the mixture becomes smoother and creamier. Add the vanilla extract and beat for a few more minutes.

9. If the mixture curdles and becomes like cottage cheese, just keep beating and it will eventually come back together.

10. Reduce the speed to low and beat for 5 minutes. This will remove most of the air bubbles.

11. Transfer to a piping bag and use it to decorate cakes, cookies, cupcakes or to fill macarons.

CHOCOLATE FROSTING

This frosting can transform any simple cake into cake heaven. There isn't anyone who tried this on one of my cakes and did not come back asking for more.

INGREDIENTS

1⅔ cups (255g) semi-sweet chocolate chips

1½ cups (339g) unsalted butter, softened

2 Tbsp. full fat milk

1 tsp. vanilla extract

2¼ cups (281g) powdered sugar, sifted

DIRECTIONS

1. Melt the chocolate in a heatproof bowl in the microwave in 30 second intervals (Start with 30 seconds, stir the chocolate, heat for another 30 seconds, and so on until the chocolate has almost fully melted). Set aside to cool.

2. In the bowl of a stand mixer fitted with the paddle attachment, cream the butter for about 3-4 minutes until pale and fluffy.

3. Add the milk and mix.

4. Add the melted chocolate and mix until well combined.

5. Add the vanilla extract and mix.

6. Add the powdered sugar gradually beating on low speed at first until they are combined. Then beat on high speed for 4-5 minutes before reducing the speed to the lowest and letting it mix for 5 minutes. This will help remove most of the air bubbles.

CHOCOLATE GANACHE

This is one of the most requested recipes from me every day. I use it very frequently for cake drips, cake fillings, tarts, and macaron fillings. It can be literally added to any dessert as a filling or topping.

INGREDIENTS

1⅔ cups (255g) semi-sweet chocolate chips
(or any chocolate chips)
1 cup (240ml) whipping cream

DIRECTIONS

1. Place the semi-sweet chocolate chips in a heatproof bowl.

2. In a small saucepan, place the whipping cream over medium heat and let it heat without stirring. Take it off the heat before it reaches the boiling. It is important that the cream is hot enough to melt the chocolate.

3. Pour the hot cream over the chocolate chips and set aside for 2 minutes without stirring.

4. Stir using a rubber spatula until you reach the desired consistency.

TIPS & TRICKS

*The ganache can be used almost immediately as cake drip. To test the consistency, run a bit of the ganache down a glass cup.

*If the ganache is being used as a tart filling, let it set for some time. If it is being used as a cake or macaron filling, whip it up using an electric or stand mixer until it thickens into a pipeable consistency.

LEMON CURD

This works as a great filling with many cake flavors. Anything lemon flavored. like a lemon cake or a lemon blueberry cake, would taste delicious with this recipe. It can be made in advance and stored in the fridge until you are ready to fill your cake.

INGREDIENTS

⅔ cup (135g) sugar

zest of 1 lemon

4 egg yolks

⅓ cup (80ml) lemon juice

pinch of salt

⅜ cup (85g) unsalted butter, softened

DIRECTIONS

1. In the bowl of a stand mixer, add the sugar, lemon zest, egg yolks, lemon juice, and salt.

2. Place a medium saucepan filled with 1 inch of water and let it simmer. Place the mixer bowl on top. Make sure the bottom of the bowl does not touch the water.

3. Whisk until combined. Whisk continuously until the mixture thickens. This will take around 10 minutes.

4. Remove the pan from the heat. Add the cubed butter and whisk.

5. Pour into a jar. Cover with a plastic wrap that covers the surface tightly so a skin does not form at the top.

6. Let it cool and then cover and refrigerate until it is ready to use.

7. Lemon curd can be made in advance and stored in the fridge.

CARAMEL SAUCE

This sauce is the perfect addition when making a caramel buttercream; however, it is equally perfect for using as a drip for cakes, as an ice cream topping, or even a topping for simple cakes.

INGREDIENTS

1 cup (200g) sugar

1/3 cup (85g) salted butter, softened at room
   temperature

¼ cup (60ml) cream , at room temperature

1 tsp. vanilla extract

¼ tsp. salt (for salted caramel)

DIRECTIONS

1. In a medium saucepan, heat the sugar over medium heat, whisking regularly until all the sugar melts.

2. Once it is dissolved, stop whisking and let it heat up until it reaches a deep golden amber color. If the sugar crystalizes, keep going and the sugar will dissolve eventually. Once the sugar dissolves and reaches the golden amber color, add the butter carefully (keeping your face away). Whisk and then remove from the heat.

3. Add the cream slowly and carefully while whisking.

4. Add the vanilla (and salt for a salted caramel sauce).

5. Let it cool for 10-15 minutes. Pour into a jar and let cool completely.

6. This caramel sauce can be stored in the fridge for up to 3 weeks. Warm slightly before using.

CARAMEL POPCORN

When I make a batch of my Homemade Caramel Popcorn recipe, I literally start putting this on everything: donuts, cupcakes, cakes and even eating and serving them to my guests as snacks. This recipe will surely impress and results in a great topping for your desserts.

INGREDIENTS

½ cup popcorn seeds

1½ cups (33g) dark brown sugar

½ cup (158ml) light corn syrup

¾ cup (170g) unsalted butter

½ tsp. baking soda

1 tsp. vanilla extract

½ tsp. salt

DIRECTIONS

1. Preheat the oven to 200°F (90°C).

2. Line a baking sheet with parchment paper.

3. Pop the popcorn kernels and place in a bowl.

4. In a medium saucepan, melt the sugar, corn syrup, and butter. Stir with a wooden spoon. Once melted, let the mixture boil for 5 minutes. Remove off the heat immediately. Be careful as the mixture is hot and bubbly.

5. Add the baking soda, vanilla, and salt and mix.

6. Pour the caramel over the popcorn and coat using a rubber spatula.

7. Once coated well, spread the popcorn evenly in the prepared baking sheet.

8. Bake for 1 hour, stirring every 20 minutes. Let the popcorn cool before placing on a cake.

9. The popcorn will keep fresh in an airtight container at room temperature for 1 week.

HOMEMADE CUSTARD

A childhood favorite! Custard can be eaten on its own or used as a filling in cakes, tarts, and cold desserts such as tiramisu. In this book, I used it in the coconut custard cake, éclairs, profiteroles, and tiramisu. To turn it into pastry cream, all you have to do is lighten it up with some whipping cream (check next recipe!).

INGREDIENTS

2 cups (480ml) full fat milk

1 Tbsp. vanilla extract

⅔ cup (133g) sugar

pinch of salt

¼ cup (30g) cornstarch

6 egg yolks

1 Tbsp. (14g) unsalted butter

DIRECTIONS

1. In a medium saucepan over medium heat, add the milk and vanilla. Bring to a boil by whisking every few minutes. As soon as the mixture boils, turn off the heat and set aside.

2. In the bowl of a stand mixer fitted with the whisk attachment, add the sugar, salt, and cornstarch. Whisk for few seconds.

3. Add the egg yolks and whisk until lighter in color.

4. Add ¼ cup of the hot milk to temper the mixture. Whisk at low speed until combined.

5. Add the remaining hot milk and mix until combined.

6. Pour the egg yolk mixture back to the saucepan passing it through a fine sieve.

7. Heat over medium heat whisking continuously until the mixture thickens and just begins to boil. Remove from the heat and add the tablespoon of butter.

8. If making in advance, cover with plastic wrap pressed tightly on the surface to prevent a skin from forming. Chill in the fridge.

PASTRY CREAM

Pastry cream can be used in so many dessert recipes, including tarts, éclairs, choux pastry, tiramisu, and even donuts. Here is a foolproof recipe that you can easily master.

INGREDIENTS

2 cups (480ml) full fat milk

1 Tbsp. vanilla extract

⅔ cup (133g) sugar

¼ cup (30g) cornstarch

6 egg yolks

1 Tbsp. unsalted butter

1 cup (240ml) whipping cream

2 Tbsp. (14g) powdered sugar

DIRECTIONS

1. In a medium saucepan over medium heat, add the milk and vanilla. Bring to a boil by whisking every few minutes. As soon as the mixture boils, turn off the heat and set aside.

2. In the bowl of a stand mixer fitted with the whisk attachment, add the sugar, salt, and cornstarch. Whisk for few seconds.

3. Add the egg yolks and whisk until lighter in color.

4. Add ¼ cup of the hot milk to temper the mixture. Whisk at low speed until combined.

5. Add the remaining hot milk and mix until combined.

6. Pour the egg yolk mixture back to the saucepan passing it through a fine sieve.

7. Heat over medium heat whisking continuously until the mixture thickens and just begins to boil. Remove from the heat and add the tablespoon of butter. This is the basic pastry cream but we will lighten it up with whipping cream.

8. If making in advance, cover with plastic wrap that is pressed tightly on the surface to prevent a skin from forming. Chill in the fridge.

9. Place a large bowl in the freezer for 5 minutes. Then using an electric mixer, whisk the cream and powdered sugar for 5 minutes until you get firm peaks.

10. Take the pastry cream made in advance out of the fridge and break it up using a whisk until the texture is creamy and smooth.

11. Add one tablespoon of the whipped cream mixture and fold it in using a spatula. Add the rest of the whipped cream and fold it into the custard to create a light and creamy pastry cream.

MASCARPONE FROSTING

This is another delicious frosting that can be used as a topping for one-layer cakes or as a filling for multi-layer cakes. It is also used in several recipes in this book, such as tiramisu.

INGREDIENTS

1 cup (227g) mascarpone cheese

1 Tbsp. vanilla extract

1 cup whipping cream

1 cup powdered sugar

DIRECTIONS

1. In the bowl of a stand mixer fitted with the paddle attachment, beat the mascarpone cheese on medium speed for 2 minutes.

2. Add the vanilla and beat.

3. Reduce the speed to low and add the whipping cream. Beat for 2-3 minutes until the frosting becomes light and fluffy.

4. Spread on cakes as a filling or use in the tiramisu recipe.

CREATING SHOWSTOPPING CAKES

Now that you have all the delicious recipes, it is time to focus on how to create cakes that not only taste delicious but also look beautiful and impressive. We will cover all the basics from trimming cake layers to the final decorating touches. Let's get started!

The first step in creating a beautiful cake is all about having a good cake recipe, a recipe that creates even cake layers that, when trimmed, have beautiful flat tops. Throughout every cake recipe in this book, I always indicated that the cake batter should be divided evenly among the prepared cake pans. To divide the cake batter evenly, put an empty cake pan on the kitchen scale then press until the weight goes to 0. If dividing into 3 pans, pour about a third of the cake batter and check the

amount measured. Now, put another empty cake pan, press the scale back to 0 and pour the exact same amount of batter as the amount measured in the first pan. Repeat with the final cake pan. This will ensure that each cake layer is the exact same size as the next.

The second important step is the right baking technique. Cakes are usually best baked at 350°F (180°C), and you will see that temperature called for throughout most of the cake recipes in this book. You can also invest in an oven thermometer to check if your oven temperature is accurate so you can adjust the temperature accordingly.

Baking strips are definitely useful. When used, they result in almost flat tops and the sides do not get a brown color. However, they do add an extra step in the baking process, and some people, including myself, prefer to skip this. As long as the recipe is good, the cake top can be easily trimmed to result in a perfectly flat cake layer.

I always store cake layers in the fridge after baking and cooling because this helps the cakes become firmer for the stacking and decoration steps. I have heard that some bakers even prefer to freeze their cake layers, but chilling the recipes provided in this book is more than enough to help you in the decorating process.

To trim the cake tops, use a serrated (bread) knife. First place a tall ruler parallel to the cake layer, Use the ruler to measure the height at which you want to cut your cake top and go around leaving a knife mark all around the circumference of the cake. This will help ensure you are cutting at the same height throughout the cake. Use the marks made on the cake and start by first just cutting the edges (do not go deep for the first round). Then start going slowly and carefully in the center as you cut round and round. Make sure not to cut too deep in the cake; the marks will help prevent this. You can save cake scraps for cake pops or cakesicles.

Stack the cake layers on top of each other to decide which layer will be first, second, third, and so on. Then place them on a wire rack to start stacking.

You will need a cake turntable. If you are skeptical about whether you need this, I assure you that it's worth the investment if you want to decorate cakes. First place a nonslip mat on top of the turntable. Then place a cake board 2 inches wider than the cake size. For example, if the cake is 6 inches across, place an 8-inch cake board on top of the nonslip mat. Pipe about a tablespoon of buttercream and smooth it with a spatula. Place another cake board the exact same size of the cake and pipe another tablespoon of buttercream. The larger cake board will help you handle the cake without smudging it later on when it has been frosted. Place the first cake layer bottom side down.

To fill each cake layer evenly, there are two options. You can either fill a piping bag and pipe a circle starting from the center of the cake and going outward until you reach the edges. Then you can smooth it out slightly with an offset spatula. This is the technique I use almost all of the time. Another technique is measuring the filling in a measuring cup. For example, if the cake is 6 inches across, measure ½ cup of buttercream or filling and spread it between each cake layer. This will ensure the filling is even among the cake layers and will result in beautiful cake guts later on when you cut the cake. If you are using a soft filling such as jam or a curd, make sure to first spread a thin layer of buttercream on the cake and pipe a ring of buttercream around the edges. Then place the soft filling in the center.

When you are filling and smoothing buttercream between cake layers, always go down to eye level with the cake to make sure the cake is looking flat and not leaning. If it is leaning on one side, use your hand to push that side downward. Having flat cake layers will make it easier to have a flat cake top later on.

Another tip that has helped transform my cakes is switching to Swiss meringue buttercream. You don't have to switch if you prefer another buttercream, such as American buttercream. However, the glossy and smooth texture of Swiss meringue buttercream results in beautiful looking cakes every single time.

Do not skip the crumb coating step. After filling the cake layers, cover the cake with a thin layer of buttercream (the "crumb coat") and smooth it out with a tall metal cake scraper. This will lock in the cake crumbs and prevent them from getting into the buttercream in the final layer of frosting.

To get sharp edges (flat cake tops and smooth cake sides), I use acrylic discs. The acrylic disc should ideally be ¼ inch wider than the cake. For example, if the cake is 6 inches across, the acrylic disc should be 6¼ inches. I wrap the acrylic disc in "press and seal" plastic wrap. This ensures that it does not smudge the cake top when it is removed later on. Before placing the acrylic disc, place a generous amount of frosting on the top of the cake and smooth it out using an offset spatula all the way until it overflows to the sides of the cake. Then place the acrylic disc and position it at the top. Start spreading the buttercream on the sides of the cake using an offset spatula. You may use a small or large offset spatula depending on what you are more comfortable with. Always spread buttercream in a parallel direction (horizontal) to the bottom of the cake and not up and down the cake. Be sure to cover all the cake as evenly as possible and then use a large cake scraper to smooth the sides. Imagine the cake is a clock. Start around the 4 o'clock position and smooth the sides in one full circle motion. Stop again at the 4 o'clock position. Do not stop in between the full circle as this will create ridges on the cake. The scraping should be with very light pressure. Always remember that you are just smoothing the sides and not trying to scrape off buttercream. After the first smoothing cycle, check the gaps on the side of the cake and fill those up with some buttercream. Then go again and, using the same technique described above, do another scraping of the cake. Continue doing this until you are happy with the result.

On some days, buttercream will be perfect, and you will not need to do anything beyond this. If you want to smooth out the cake even more, you can heat the metal scraper with a kitchen torche or hot water and do a final smoothing of the cake sides. I call this "ironing out" the cake because it produces such a beautiful and smooth cake.

Chill the cake for at least one hour before attempting to remove the acrylic disc. To remove the acrylic disc, you can use a thread. Cut out a long piece of thread. Then, pass the thread carefully and gently in between the acrylic disc and the top of the cake. Start from the side of the cake facing you and go all the way to the other side. This will help lift off the acrylic disc without ruining the cake top. Remove the acrylic disc by pulling up the "press and seal" paper at the top.

Now that you've got a beautiful cake base, it is time to decorate. There are so many different techniques to decorating buttercream cakes, but here are a few ideas to inspire you when you are creating your next cake:

- Pipe a simple rope border at the top (Wilton 1M piping tip works best for this).
- Pipe a rope border at the top and bottom of the cake using Wilton 1M or a French star tip such as Wilton 4B or 6B.
- Pipe ice cream style swirls all around the cake top. First pipe 4 swirls at the 3, 6, 9, and 12 o'clock positions. Then pipe in between these swirls to fill the gaps.
- Use a combed cake scraper to create a simple design or be adventurous and use a striped cake comb to create cake stripes. The best way to create cake stripes is to pipe an even layer of buttercream around the cake then scrape the sides using the comb. If there are gaps, you can fill these up with the same buttercream color and scrape again until it is even. Make sure you always use the same side of the comb that you used for creating the stripes first. Chill the cake for at least one hour, the longer the better, before filling the stripes with another color. After chilling, fill the stripes with the chosen color(s). It is best if the colors are in piping bags with piping tips the exact size of the stripe gaps. Then, smooth the cake sides again and again until the stripes appear and are as clean as possible.
- Fill various colors of buttercream in piping bags with the following tips (Wilton 1M, 4B, 6B, 106) and pipe stars, rosettes, and wiggles on the cake partially or the entire cake.

- Cut out fondant (sugar paste) shapes using any chosen cookie cutter. Let the fondant shapes dry in open air overnight and then use buttercream to stick them unto the cake. For example, you can cut out hearts from fondant and use them to cover an entire cake. They can be the same color, ombre colors, or several different colors.

- Color buttercream different colors (example: rainbow colors) and then fill each color in a piping bag fitted with a petal tip (example: Wilton 104 piping tip). Start piping ruffles from the cake top going round and round until you reach the bottom. Make each ruffle a different color.

- You can also use silicone molds and fondant to create beautiful shapes and apply them on the cake again using buttercream.

Other beautiful touches that can be added to any cake design include sprinkles, glitter, sugar, high quality edible gold leaf, mini macarons, fresh florals, and wafer paper.

To get inspiration on colors that go well together, look around you or online at various images of nature, art, fashion, and so on. You will get an idea of which colors go best together.

A final tip that makes a huge difference in how your final cake looks is the cake board/drum being used. Silver cake drums are no longer in style, and they may make your beautiful cake that you worked on so hard on appear old fashioned. Replace silver cake drums with either white, gold, or colorful cake drums that are widely available. You can even serve your cake directly on the cake stand. Make sure the cake is well chilled and use a cake lifter to lift the cake directly onto the cake stand.

INDEX

ABOUT THE AUTHOR

Chahrazad is the baker, photographer, and creator behind her famous desserts page "Chahrazad's Cuisine", established in 2013 where she creates tutorials that make baking look easy and fun. Chahrazad shares her dessert creations and teaches the art of baking to audiences from all over the world. She has over 3.5 million followers on Tiktok, 175k on Instagram, and 180k subscribers on Youtube. In 2020, she also launched her own Sprinkles line, called Pinkles.

Chahrazad regularly appears on regional and local TV channels in Dubai and in April of 2021 she hosted her first own cooking show. She also regularly shoots campaigns for famous global and regional brands across the food industry. Chahrazad lives in Dubai with her husband and 2 kids. When she is not baking in the kitchen, she loves to host friends over delicious meals, read or watch the famous Friends sitcom.